EA Principals'

40 TOGAF® 9.1 Certification Level 2 Practice Scenarios Volume 1

PREFACE

Why is this book necessary? For one thing, no other such book exists. There is no source – anywhere, in any form or format – that provides a comprehensive set of exams to provide practice in taking the TOGAF® 9.1 Level 2 Certification Examination.

This is a unique offering because it includes 5 complete practice exams for Level 2 in one book.

The reasons for TOGAF's rising popularity are many and varied. Good luck in soon joining the community of over 20,000 TOGAF Certified Enterprise Architects.

1. First and foremost, TOGAF has proven itself to be an effective industry standard framework and method for enterprise architecture. TOGAF succeeds in effectively aligning Business systems and processes, the data and information needed to facilitate business operations, the applications that manipulate the data/information for business use, and the technology on which the applications and data/information reside.

2. TOGAF is complementary to, not competing with, other architecture frameworks. TOGAF is not "either-or" – it can be "both-and."

3. Similarly, TOGAF can be used in conjunction with other, non-architecture standards and methodologies. Examples include the Baldrige Criteria for Performance Excellence, various ISO standards, the EA Kanban Board, the Government Performance and Results Act requirements and other strategic planning frameworks, and various dashboards and "balanced measures" approaches.

4. TOGAF provides a repository of best practices. As such TOGAF both promotes knowledge capture, sharing, and management within the enterprise while at the same time demystifying Enterprise Architecture.

5. TOGAF is vendor-, tool-, and technology-neutral. As an example, TOGAF can be used in an organization's Application Architecture, irrespective of, say, the particular Customer Relationship Management application used by the organization.

6. TOGAF is not a "one size fits all" approach to enterprise architecture. TOGAF is tailorable, and can therefore be used in a wide variety of types and sizes of organizations.

TOGAF is a framework and method for achieving the vision of "Boundaryless Information Flow."

EA Principals, Inc., has developed these practice questions based on The Open Group conformance requirements for the TOGAF® Certification for People program. They are not official practice questions and have not been reviewed or approved by The Open Group. Official Practice questions are only available from The Open Group (see www.TOGAF.info).

The basic document used in compiling this book is *TOGAF® Version 9.1* Standard, referred to as "The Book" (ISBN: 978 90 8753 679 4, G116), available at www.opengroup.org/bookstore/catalog/g116.htm. The Book is also available in abbreviated/outline form online at www.opengroup.org/architecture/TOGAF9-doc/arch.

Boundaryless Information Flow™ is a trademark and ArchiMate®, Jericho Forum®, Making

Standards Work®, Motif®, OSF/1®, The Open Group®, TOGAF®, UNIX®, and the ``X'' device are registered trademarks of The Open Group in the United States and other countries. All other brand, company, and product names are used for identification purposes only and may be trademarks that are the sole property of their respective owners.

Table of Contents

Overview

THE OPEN GROUP

According to its web page (http://www.theopengroup.org/aboutus), The Open Group is a global consortium that enables the achievement of business objectives through IT standards. The Open Group includes more than 400 member organizations, with a diverse membership that spans all sectors of the global economy — customers, systems and solutions suppliers, tool vendors, integrators and consultants, as well as academics and researchers.

The Open Group Mission Statement states that the mission of The Open Group is to drive the creation of Boundaryless Information Flow™ by: working with customers to capture, understand, and address current and emerging requirements, establishing policies, and sharing best practices; working with suppliers, consortia, and standards bodies to develop consensus and facilitate interoperability, to evolve and integrate specifications and open source technologies; offering a comprehensive set of services to enhance the operational efficiency of consortia; and developing and operating the industry's premier certification service and encouraging procurement of certified products.

TOGAF® TRAINING

This book is meant to be a supplement to – in no way a substitute for – formal TOGAF® training courses, rigorous self-study, and hands-on application and implementation of TOGAF®. Mastery of the "practice scenarios" included herein is no guarantee that the reader will pass the TOGAF® 9 Level 2 certification examination. There is no substitute for formal TOGAF® training, conducted by a training organization that has been accredited by The Open Group, and actual experience applying TOGAF®. Formal TOGAF® training is conducted by a number of organizations, including EA Principals, Inc. That training is meant to prepare students to pass the TOGAF® Level 1 (Foundation) or Level 2 (Certified) certification exam, or both.

TOGAF® CERTIFICATION EXAMINATIONS

The Level 1 and Level 2 examinations are very different. While both examinations are multiple-choice, the approaches taken by the respective exams are different. For example, Level 1 questions are pretty much objective, and deal with basic concepts and components of TOGAF®; questions in the Level 1 examination require understanding of the Components of TOGAF®, in particular the Architecture Development Method. Level 2 questions require in-depth understanding of how to apply TOGAF®; the questions ask how you would apply TOGAF® in a scenario to improve a situation or to resolve an issue.

The Level 1 examination is closed-book; you may not use any reference materials or notes. The Level 2 examination is open-book; a PDF version of the TOGAF® 9 Standard will be provided for your use during the examination. That said, because of the length of the TOGAF® Standard, and because of the time limit imposed for taking the examination, few test-takers have the time to actually use the Standard during the examination.

In the Level 2 examination, there are eight questions (worth a possible total of 40 points), each having four possible answers. Each question describes a scenario, in which a problem or issue is raised. This is followed by a question that puts you into the role of an Architect, and asks how you would respond to the problem or issue – using TOGAF®. Then, four possible courses of action are presented. One of the courses of action is the "best" course of action; it is worth five points. Another course is next-best, and is worth three points. A third course of action is least-best and is worth one point. The final course of action is a "distractor" – it can do nothing to resolve the issue presented in the scenario, or it has nothing to do with TOGAF® – and is worth zero points. You will need a minimum of 24 points (60%) to pass the Level 2 examination.

TIPS FOR TAKING THE LEVEL 2 EXAMINATION

There are a number of factors that will help you pass the Level 2 examination.

One proven approach for taking the Level 2 examination begins with achieving a thorough understanding of how to apply TOGAF®. First and foremost, there is no substitute for good training. Be sure to take a TOGAF® training course from a training organization that has been accredited by The Open Group. The "accredited" part is very important: Accreditation tells you that a training organization has undergone a rigorous evaluation by The Open Group and has been found to be in full compliance with all of The Open Group's quality and accreditation requirements.

Experience: If you are in a position to acquire hands-on experience implementing, applying, or managing a TOGAF® system, this will be of great benefit. If you are not in such a position, a brief assignment to your Enterprise Architecture department could be one way to acquire experience.

Becoming "test savvy": Knowing the structure of the examination and how to attack the questions is often the key to success in taking a test. The first of these topics is addressed in the preceding section; the second, how to attack the questions, is addressed below. It is important to know that, unlike some examinations, the TOGAF® certification examinations do not impose a penalty for incorrect responses. Accordingly, answer all questions – even if you have to guess.

Practice: The practice scenarios in this book are similar to the types of scenarios you will see on the TOGAF® Level 2 examination. Use these practice scenarios to both know more about the examination, and to increase your understanding of TOGAF®. Please don't simply memorize the correct answers and expect to see the same questions on the examination. Understanding why the correct answers are correct is the key to successful use of this book. Using practice scenarios also helps with the next factor – time management. The scenarios in this book are divided into five sets of eight scenarios each. Use the five sets as practice examinations; time yourself to make sure you can finish in the required 90 minutes.

Time Management: The TOGAF® Level 2 examination is timed – you will be allowed 90 minutes to complete the examination. You will not be allowed to take your wristwatch (or anything else) into the examination with you. But there will be a "Time Remaining" clock on your computer screen when you take the exam. Pay attention to it!

Should you answer each question before moving to the next one? If that is how you take tests, then by all means use that approach. But remember: the more time you spend on one question, the less you will have to spend on the others. Also remember that you may skip questions and go back and answer them later. You may also go back and change your answers at any time before you either press the "Complete" button or you run out of time. Most Candidates who take the TOGAF® examinations go through the examination several times. First, they answer the questions that they are sure about. Then they answer the ones they are not quite sure about, and then the ones they really are not sure about. Then they guess on the ones about which they have no clue. When dealing with the questions they are not quite sure about or really not sure about, they first try to identify and eliminate the "distractor." Then they put the other three answers in order of how well they would address the issue presented in the scenario. Then they pick the one that would add most value to the issue resolution.

Taking both Level 1 and Level 2 examinations in "Combined" mode: While both Level 1 and Level 2 examinations can be taken in a Combined examination, we do not recommend this. The most important reason is that a huge mental paradigm shift is required when going from the Level 1 examination format to the Level 2 format. In particular, the Level 1 examination requires more linear, "left-brain" thinking, while the Level 2 examination requires more complex, "right-brain" approaches to issues and problems. We recommend that candidates study for the Level 1 examination, pass the examination, and then spend some time studying for the Level 2 examination to get into the right "mind-set" for that examination.

Using This Book

This book is conveniently divided into five sets of eight scenarios each. This allows the student to simulate taking the Level 2 test five separate times in five separate sittings. It is recommended that the student settle into a quiet location and block off 90 minutes of uninterrupted time. Then use a section of eight scenarios for self-testing. The answer keys are at the end of each set of scenarios. You may also create additional practice examinations by mixing scenarios from the five sets. When answering each scenario, the student should not only try to find the best answer, but also attempt to determine the second-best, third-best, and the distractor.

Other EA Principals Products and Services

In addition to this book, EA Principals, Inc., offers a companion volume of 1600 practice questions to help candidates prepare to take the TOGAF® Level 1 (Foundation) examination.

EA Principals also provides TOGAF® training courses to provide the knowledge required to pass the Level 1 and Level 2 examinations. These courses can be taken as private courses (i.e., presented at your organization – and specifically tailored to meet your organization's unique requirements) or public courses (presented at a central training facility and open to students from any organization). These courses can also be presented on line via webinar. For individuals who are Level 2 certified, but wish to achieve a higher level of TOGAF® expertise, EA Principals also offers both Advanced Applied TOGAF and Advanced Applied ArchiMate.

EA Principals also offers courses in the Department of Defense Architecture Framework (DoDAF) and the Federal/Federated Enterprise Architecture Framework (FEAF), and will soon offer training in the Zachman Framework. Related training offered by EA Principals includes (or will soon include) such diverse topics as Business Architecture, Business Analysis, Project Management, Knowledge Management, and Organizational Performance Assessment and Improvement.

Finally, EA Principals offers on-site assistance, coaching, and mentoring in all of the topics mentioned above. View the complete catalogue of offerings at www.eaprincipals.com.

Set 1: Scenarios 1 - 8

SCENARIO #1 Visum Futurum ST, Inc.

BACKGROUND

Visum Futurum ST, Inc. (VFST) is a privately funded space exploration venture developing long-range strategic initiatives for human exploration and colonization of space. They are presently focused on the Moon and Mars for scientific settlements tailored after the models used for research in the Antarctic. The corporation is a closely-knit affiliation of several entities each with its own specified function in the program. The entire affiliation uses a central shared IT infrastructure that is ultimately managed by an executive triad called "Tri-IT": CFO, CIO, and COO, with the CFO as the lead. The company has a solid TOGAF® Enterprise Architecture team that has built and maintained the information systems frameworks from VFST's inauguration.

The firm is about to begin preparations for its first live mission: the building of a layover space station to act as a transition point between suborbital and extra-orbital flight. The Tri-IT executives have recently evaluated the functional capabilities of the IT support systems to handle the expected large volume of data transactions, communications, and application usage from the affiliations. Their findings concluded that the present systems are inadequate to handle the expected load. They believe that the IT systems undergo a fundamental restructuring and have decided on transitioning their current server-based data center model to the more flexible cloud computing model.

The Request for Architecture and Architecture Vision are complete and the Architecture Development Iteration is ready to proceed. But there are some concerns: the CIO and COO are in a disagreement about which architecture should lead the transition program: Data and Application (CIO), or Technology (COO); the head of Software Engineering is concerned about loss of access to systems and applications during the transition; and the CEO wants to be assured that the transition carefully identifies how each element of the solution will impact the functioning of current projects.

QUESTION

Refer to the scenario

Your role is the Chief Architect.

You have been asked to present to the Tri-IT the baseline architecture of the current systems before moving into the target architecture iteration of the Architecture Development Cycle. Based on TOGAF® 9, which of the following is the best answer?

ANSWERS

A. During Phase B, use an Organization/Actor catalog, a Driver/Goal/Objective Catalog, a Location Catalog, and a Business Interaction Matrix; in Phase C: Data Architecture, use a Data Entity/Data Component Catalog, a Data Entity/Business Function Matrix, and a Logical Data Diagram; in Phase C: Application Architecture, create an Application Portfolio Catalog, an Application/Organization Matrix, an Application Use-Case Diagram, an Enterprise

Manageability Diagram, a Software Engineering Diagram; in Phase D, use a Technology Standards Catalog, a Technology Portfolio Catalog, a Platform Decomposition Diagram, a Networked Computing/Hardware Diagram, and a Communications Engineering Diagram.

B. During Phase D, use a Technology Standards Matrix, a Technology Systems Catalog, a Environments and Locations Diagram, a Networked Computing/Hardware Diagram, and a Technology Construction Engineering Diagram; in Phase B, use an Organization/Actor catalog, a Role Catalog, a Location Catalog, and a Process/Event/Control/Product Catalog; in Phase C: Data Architecture, use a Data Entity/Data Component Catalog, a Data Entity/Business Function Matrix, and a Data Phase Gate Diagram; last, in Phase C: Application Architecture, create a Value Chain Diagram, an Application/Organization Matrix, an Application Interaction Matrix, and a Solution Concept Diagram.

C. During Phases B and C, use an Organization/Actor catalog, a Driver/Goal/Objective Catalog, a Location Catalog, and a Business Interaction Matrix, a Data Entity/Data Component Catalog, a Data Entity/Business Function Matrix, a Logical Data Diagram, an Application Portfolio Catalog, an Application/Organization Matrix, an Application Use-Case Diagram, an Enterprise Manageability Diagram, a Software Engineering Diagram; in Phase D, use a Technology Standards Catalog, a Technology Portfolio Catalog, a Platform Decomposition Diagram, a Networked Computing/Hardware Diagram, and a Communications Engineering Diagram.

D. During Phase B, use an Organization/Actor catalog, a Role Catalog, a Location Catalog, and a Process/Event/Control/Product Catalog; in Phase C: Data Architecture, use a Data Entity/Data Component Catalog, a Data Entity/Business Function Matrix, and a Data Security Diagram; in Phase C: Application Architecture, create an Application Portfolio Catalog, an Application/Organization Matrix, an Application Interaction Matrix, and an Enterprise Manageability Diagram; in Phase D, use a Technology Standards Catalog, a Technology Portfolio Catalog, a Environments and Locations Diagram, a Networked Computing/Hardware Diagram, and a Communications Engineering Diagram.

SCENARIO #2 SoCal Bank

BACKGROUND

SoCal Bank, a high profile financial services subsidiary of Burgan-Morgan Finance, was enduring significant computing and financial inefficiencies via server sprawl. They were managing distributed server environments that were spread across the country, the current environment was difficult to manage and costly. The distributed systems were a result of 2 factors: 1) mergers and acquisitions, and 2) uneven use of technology between business units. The culture at SoCal has had its emphasis on services without the appropriate concerns for technology and architecture framework. Burgan-Morgan saw significant lack of increase in profitability of SoCal in comparison to more technically flexible subsidiaries. An initial review discovered a very inefficient process infrastructure with unnecessary expenses due to a lack of communication between the business and technology organizations.

The Board of Directors of Burgan-Morgan decided to extend their EA team and assign them to SoCal to institute a structured framework for enterprise architecture to reduce the expenses and increase the capabilities of SoCal. The EA team met with both the Burgan-Morgan Board and SoCal executives to initiate discussions on transitioning the latter to a solid architecture framework. This was followed by an iteration of the Preliminary Phase where the scope included a strong focus on the issues surrounding the uncoordinated communications between the technology and business organizations. The Request for Architecture Work was completed and the ADM cycle was initiated.

QUESTION

Refer to the scenario

Your role is the Chief Architect. During the course of creating the Architecture Vision, how would you best focus on the concerns of the stakeholders, based on TOGAF® 9?

ANSWERS

A. Develop Process Modeling Extensions: Create events as triggers for processes; create controls that business logic and governance gates for process execution; create event diagrams. Develop Data Extensions: create logical data components that group data entities into encapsulated modules for governance, security, and deployment services; create physical data components that implement logical data components and are analogous to databases, registries, repositories, schemas, and other techniques of segmenting data; create a data lifecycle, data security, and data migration diagrams of the architecture to show data concerns in more detail.

B. Develop Governance Extensions: establish measures to objectives and link them to services; apply contracts to service communication with external users and systems; define re-usable services qualities with a service level profile to be used in contracts; create additional diagrams to show ownership and management of systems. Develop Services Extensions: create an Information Systems service as an extension to business service to establish solid communications between the business and application architectures. Develop Motivation Extensions: create a Driver metamodel entity to identify factors motivating or constraining the organization; create a Goal metamodel entity to establish strategic purpose and mission; create an Objective metamodel entity to show near to mid-term achievements; create a Goal/Objective/Service diagram to show traceability through these new metamodel entities.

C. Develop Governance Extensions: establish measures to objectives and link them to services; apply contracts to service communication with external users and systems; define re-usable services qualities with a service level profile to be used in contracts; create additional diagrams to show ownership and management of systems. Develop Process Modeling Extensions: Create events as triggers for processes; create controls that business logic and governance gates for process execution; create event diagrams. Develop Motivation Extensions: create a Driver metamodel entity to identify factors motivating or constraining the organization; create a Goal metamodel entity to establish strategic purpose and mission; create an Objective metamodel entity to show near to mid-term achievements; create a Goal/Objective/Service diagram to show traceability through these new metamodel entities.

D. Develop Governance Extensions: establish measures to objectives and link them to services; apply contracts to service communication with external users and systems; define re-usable services qualities with a service level profile to be used in contracts; create additional diagrams to show ownership and management of systems. Develop Services Extensions: create an Information Systems service as an extension to business service to establish solid communications between the business and application architectures. Develop Data Extensions: create logical data components that group data entities into encapsulated modules for governance, security, and deployment services; create a data lifecycle, data security, and data migration diagrams of the architecture to show data concerns in more detail.

SCENARIO #3 Pyramid Sales

BACKGROUND

Pyramid Sales is a leading global beauty company with 100,000 plus sales leaders and millions of representatives worldwide, Pyramid Sales runs regular campaigns but reports on these were typically received too late to affect current sales activity. A single standardized platform and reporting function was needed to support global campaigns, but these needed to interact seamlessly with existing technologies and Internet portals. Pyramid Sales is looking to evolve onto a salesforce.com platform that would become integrated with Pyramid Sales' own data warehousing platform. A pilot and deployment was successfully implemented in 5 locations in Arizona. Now, at those locations, there is a twice-daily information flow from order transactions through the data warehouse to the salesforce.com portal, supported by easy to use interfaces customized to be consistent with the Pyramid Sales look and feel. There is also seamless integration with Pyramid Sales' Web portal, with single sign-on, making it easy for sales leaders to access all the information they need in one place.

Pyramid Sales has a mature Enterprise Architecture team and bases their framework on TOGAF® 9.1. Now that the pilot program is completed and deemed successful, they are moving forward with full implementation. But before the implementation begins, the CEO, along with the Board Chairmen and concurrence of the CFO, has directed that the CIO now include mobile access as part of the solution set. This called for a new Request for Architecture document and initiation of another ADM cycle. Now, a new draft Architecture Definition Document has been completed to account for this additional functionality.

QUESTION

Refer to the scenario

Your role is the Chief Architect.

You have been asked to complete the tasks necessary before preparing the final Architecture Roadmap and Implementation and Migration Plan.

Based on TOGAF® 9, which of the following is the best answer?

ANSWERS

A. Design the Implementation and Migration Plan, as well as the Architecture Repository, to transition the mobile access feature after all of the sites has been migrated to the new architecture. Doing so will greatly reduce the number of faults and rollbacks sure to be encountered. Before implementing the mobile access feature, review the gap analysis results from the Architecture Development iterations and consolidate the mobile access-related elements into the Implementation Factor Assessment Matrix. Ensure that all enterprise remote access/mobile users are trained in using the new technology before the release date. Publish Architecture Framework Catalog to the CEO for review and approval. Execute the lessons learned activities and place the results in the Architecture Repository.

B. Create an Implementation Factor Assessment and Deduction Matrix addressing the new Mobile Access requirement that will store information on implementation and migration; assess the transition capabilities of the migrating units; identify risks that may hinder the sequence of the implementation; review the Enterprise Architecture Maturity Assessment. Observe the coordination between business planning, enterprise architecture, portfolio/project management, and operations management. Assign a business value to each work package making sure to evaluate for gaps between SBBs and ABBs. Estimate resource requirements, the times needed for each project and how much each will cost. Prioritize transition projects with a cost/benefit analysis and business transformation readiness assessment. Generate the final Architecture Roadmap and Implementation and Migration Plans.

C. Create an Implementation Factor Assessment and Deduction Matrix addressing the new Mobile Access requirement that will store information on implementation and migration; assess the transition capabilities of the migrating units; identify risks that may hinder the sequence of the implementation; review the Enterprise Architecture Maturity Assessment. Identify the SBBs that would close gaps associated with their ABBs; resolve the gaps and rationalize the Consolidated Gaps, Solutions, and Dependencies Matrix; update the Implementation Factor Assessment and Deduction Matrix. Consolidate requirements across business functions and reconcile interoperability conflicts for delivering an efficient shared architecture across the enterprise. Fold the mobile access elements into the draft Implementation and Migration Plan and the draft Architecture Roadmap.

D. Review the gap analysis results from the Architecture Development iterations and consolidate the mobile access-related elements into the Implementation Factor Assessment Matrix. Ensure that all enterprise remote access/mobile users are trained in using the new technology before the release date. Order the sequence so that the mobile access capability is not rolled out until the new architecture is in place to preclude conflicting risks between the two elements. Document the draft Implementation and Migration plan, and have it follow the mandates of the Architecture Board's Architecture Roadmap. Align the new Implementation and Migration plan with the Request for Architecture Work, Architecture Vision, and Statement of Architecture documents. Establish governance criteria for the Architecture Board to review and approve.

SCENARIO #4 Portable Foundations

BACKGROUND

Portable Foundations are one of the largest pre-engineered portable steel building OEM manufacturers in North America. They have a high reputation for their portable building products and are well known for a commitment to providing their customers with the finest metal building at the lowest cost. They offer nationwide service and delivery of steel portable buildings. They supply a wide range of steel buildings from conventional steel buildings to custom-designed steel frame structures supporting brick, rock, block, stucco and concrete exteriors.

One of the company's core strengths is its ability to self-perform a large portion of fieldwork, providing optimal control over safety, cost, schedule and quality. Additionally, their in-house project managers work closely with clients and field teams to create safe, cost effective building solutions with minimal environmental impact.

Portable Foundations has grown exponentially in the past few years but has not kept up its technology infrastructure to scale up to its larger size. Instead of carefully planning a centralized technological architecture, they have settled for a distributed environment which seemed time saving during the growth period. The CFO and CIO have finished discussions about a plan to finally bring in all shared resources into two data centers. Stakeholders from manufacturing are concerned about production loss in this growth period. They believe that serial procedures will lose coordination with parallel procedures.

As the concept for the transition was being debated, OSHA published new regulations for portable building construction. The regulations would be another impact on manufacturing during the transition. However, the Board of Directors and executive teams believed that it might be advantageous to have both of these issues at the same time because production would be affected during a single period of time rather than in two consecutive programs.

Portable Foundations have hired an enterprise architecture consultancy to plan the best route to a successful transition. After meeting with the EA leads, the stakeholders expressed apprehension about the viability of the new solution to meet the regulatory requirements for portable building installations as well as the impact of rationalizing the information systems down to the agreed upon infrastructure.

QUESTION

Refer to the scenario

Your role is the Chief Architect. As part of the plans for the transition, there are certain aspects that need attention to assure the least amount of disruption.

Based on TOGAF® 9, which of the following is provides the best answer in respect to the concerns of the stakeholders?

ANSWERS

A. During Phase B create an Organization/Actor Catalog, a Driver/Goal/Objective Catalog, a location Catalog, a Process/Event/Control Product Catalog, a Process Flow Diagram, and an Event Diagram. During Phase C (Application), create a Process/Application Realization Diagram, an Application Migration Diagram, and a Software Distribution Diagram. In Phase D, create a Processing Diagram, a Networked Computing/Hardware Diagram, and a Communications Engineering Diagram. Finally, in Phase E, you develop a Project Context Diagram, complete the Gap Analysis, review consolidated requirements across related business functions, consolidate and reconcile interoperability requirements, refine and validate dependencies, formulate the Implementation and Migration Strategy, and create the Architecture Roadmap & Implementation and Migration Plan.

B. During Phase A, create extensions to the Content Metamodel. Add Event, Control, and Product extensions; create diagrams that show the way in which business functions, events, controls, and products are linked to support a particular business scenario; create diagrams that show events, were they are received from, and what processes they trigger. In Phase B, create a Process/Event/Control/Product Catalog. Create a location entity to hold the location of IT assets; create logical and physical application components to abstract the capability of applications; abstract logical and physical application components; create additional diagrams focusing on the location of assets, compliance with standards, structure of applications, application migration, and infrastructure configuration; create processing diagrams.

C. Create an initial risk assessment using the following classification criteria: Catastrophic, Critical, Marginal, and Negligible. Then create frequency classifications; Frequent, Likely, Occasional, Seldom, and Unlikely. Create a Risk Classification Scheme based on these criteria to establish whether risks are Extremely High, High Risk, Moderate Risk, and Low Risk. Associate this schema with the risk concerns of the stakeholders. Plan for risk mitigations and conduct a residual risk assessment to plan in advance problems to be faced. Modify

Architecture Governance to handle the review of the progress of the implementation to watch for risks to occur and implement change management to correct the problems. Inform the Architecture Review Board of these enhancements to insure their cognizance of the expected problem to occur as implementation plays out.

D. During Phase A, create extensions to the Content Metamodel. Create a location entity to hold the location of IT assets; create logical and physical application components to abstract the capability of applications; abstract logical and physical application components; create additional diagrams focusing on the location of assets, compliance with standards, structure of applications, application migration, and infrastructure configuration; create processing diagrams. Apply measurements to objectives and then link those measures to services; apply contracts to service interactions with external users and systems; define re-usable service qualities defining a service-level profile that can be used in contracts; create additional diagrams to show ownership and management of systems, and diagrams of system operation and dependencies on operations processes.

SCENARIO #5 Phoenix Motor Oil (PMOL)

BACKGROUND

Phoenix Motor Oil (PMOL) is a domestic manufacturer of motor oils specially produced for Formula 1 racing car engines. Last year, the company experienced a windfall from profits earned as an indirect result of a string of racing victories by their biggest customer who are now expanding their operations. PMOL had been delaying a program to establish a solid enterprise architecture just as the windfall occurred. The CEO and CFO agreed to move forward with the program. The architecture team has completed the Architecture Development and Transition Planning iterations and has now moved into the next phase.

About this time, the CFO expressed concerns about the implementation: the program, to this point, was excessively over budget mostly due to the inadequacies of the then current Chief Architect (CA). The Lead Architect was selected to continue the program but would have to present to the Architecture Board the methodology for running a smooth transition with little to no impact to the remaining budget. The former CA had failed to leave the detailed plan upon departure, so the new CA had to create one from scratch.

QUESTION

Refer to the scenario

Your role is the Chief Architect.

You have been asked to present to the Architecture Board the details of the Implementation Plan keeping in mind their concerns.

Based on TOGAF® 9, which of the following is the best answer?

ANSWERS

A. You present to the AB the following plan: At the beginning of each transition point, the AB will receive documentation providing the scope of the projects to be completed as they relate to the strategic goals set by the stakeholders. They will receive a complete list of change requests to allow them to review and analyze for their cost impacts. They will receive updated gap analyses between the solutions architecture and operations. The EA team will set up a compliance review process to: ensure that building blocks are being applied as planned, and at the end of each transition point, ensure that the project is meeting specifications established in transition planning.

B. You present to the AB the following plan: At the beginning of each transition point, the AB will receive documentation providing the scope of the projects to be completed as they relate to the strategic goals set by the stakeholders. During implementation, the EA team will update the Enterprise Continuum and Architecture Repositories with any new building blocks created during the implementation. The AB will also be tasked to run the compliance reviews. At the end of the transition, the AB will produce a report on the results of all compliance reviews for further analysis on the next project.

C. You present to the AB the following plan: At the beginning of each transition point, the AB will receive documentation providing the scope of the projects to be completed as they relate to the strategic goals set by the stakeholders. During implementation, the EA team will update the Enterprise Continuum and Architecture Repositories with any new building blocks created during the implementation. They will also set up a compliance review process to ensure that building blocks are being applied as planned, and, at the end of each transition point, ensure that the project is meeting specifications established in transition planning. After each transition, the AB will have access to all completed change request reports as well as any gaps that were encountered and resolved.

D. You present to the AB the following plan: At the beginning of each transition point, the EA team will create a new implementation plan, followed by a reorganization of the team structure. This will provide cross training among the personnel, which will insure constant communications between the implementation and operational teams. This will affect the budgetary constraints in a positive way by using the principle of Boundaryless Information Flow. At the end of the transitions, the EA team will summarize the experience in a high-level executive summary.

SCENARIO #6 eFortitude

BACKGROUND

eFortitude is a web-based financial company in business since 1995. After surviving the crash of 2000, the business has had fits and starts keeping afloat as newer online financial services start-ups flourish; the probable cause being the competition lacked baggage from pre-crash methods and procedures. In other words, they were restrained by an obsolescent culture. In the last six months, however, eFortitude shareholders replaced the entire executive board with younger, more Internet savvy individuals with a proven track record of cunning business skills. The new CEO, CFO, and CIO subsequently reduced and replaced middle managers and flattened the entire management structure. This allowed them to have a closer view into the day-to-day operations of the firm. After this six month period, they held a round-table with a cross-section of employees from VPs down to individual contributors to establish a new direction for the company that would not only rejuvenate the brand, but to become the top selling online financial institution.

The first goal they established was to rethink the technology infrastructure from the network to applications and the processes needed to accomplish a successful refresh. The new VP of IT and 3 of the employees she brought in were experienced in TOGAF® and Enterprise Architecture, having successfully conducted a similar transition in their prior company. They were immediately given the charter to conduct the migration for eFortitude.

They have just completed the Request for Architecture Work and are now about to present their plan to the shareholders. The shareholders, being unaware of Enterprise Architecture, were skeptical of their plan, which they saw as a bit too ambitious and risky. They wanted a review of the plan the EA team would employ to oversee risks in the transition.

QUESTION

Refer to the scenario

Your role is the Chief Architect.

You have completed your presentation for the shareholders. Which of the answers below would best outline your presentation?

Based on TOGAF® 9, which of the following is the best answer?

ANSWERS

A. In the Architecture Development Iteration, classify risks in terms of time, budget, and scope. Use CMMs to help identify risks imminent in the baseline and target architectures. In Phase E, establish the effect of risks in terms of catastrophic, critical, marginal, and negligible. Determine the expected frequency of the identified risks. Using that information, create a Risk Classification Scheme. In Phase F, Plan on the deployment of risk mitigation and assess the probable residual risks. In Phase G, monitor and manage the implementation, enact the mitigation of the risks as determined in Phase F.

B. In Phase A, classify risks in terms of time, budget, and scope. Use CMMs to help identify risks imminent in the baseline and target architectures. Establish the effect of risks in terms of catastrophic, critical, marginal, and negligible. Determine the expected frequency of the identified risks. Using that information, create a Risk Classification Scheme. Plan on the deployment of risk mitigation and assess the probable residual risks. In Phase G, monitor and manage the implementation, enact the mitigation of the risks as determined in Phase A.

C. In Phase A, classify risks in terms of time, budget, and scope. In the Architecture Development Iterations, use CMMs to help identify risks imminent in the baseline and target architectures. Establish the effect of risks in terms of catastrophic, critical, marginal, and negligible. Determine the expected frequency of the identified risks. Using that information, create a Risk Classification Scheme. Plan on the deployment of risk mitigation and assess the probable residual risks. In Phase G, monitor and manage the implementation, enact the mitigation of the risks as determined in Phase E.

D. In the Preliminary Phase, engage the Architecture Board to round-table a discussion of their concerns about specific risks that need to be addressed in the development of the target architecture. Create a plan for mitigating all risks; eliminate the factors that would create residual risks. In the Architecture Development Iteration, classify risks in terms of time, budget, and scope. Use CMMs to help identify risks imminent in the baseline and target architectures. In

Phases E and F, establish the effect of risks in terms of catastrophic, critical, marginal, and negligible. Determine the expected frequency of the identified risks. Using that information, create a Risk Classification Scheme. Plan on the deployment of risk mitigation and assess the probable residual risks.

SCENARIO #7 Government Accounting Agency (GAO)

BACKGROUND

The Government Accounting Agency (GAO) conducted an audit of Army and Air Force Business (AAFB) systems, which resulted in the following report.

Assessments by independent government agencies identified operational problems, such as deficiencies in data accuracy, inability to generate auditable financial reports, and the need for manual workarounds. Further, according to Defense Finance and Accounting Services (DFAS) users, the AAFB did not provide all expected capabilities in accounting and decision support.

To help provide for the successful implementation of Army and Air Force ERPs, GAO recommended that the Secretary of Defense should direct that the Milestone Decision Authority (MDA) ensure that any future system deficiencies identified through independent assessments are resolved or mitigated prior to further deployment of the systems.

QUESTION

Refer to the scenario

You are the Chief Architect recently contracted by the Milestone Decision Authority to apply TOGAF® methodologies that will satisfy the requirements of the GAO. TOGAF® is not currently in use for the agencies involved. Your first task is to establish an enterprise architecture team and prepare to begin the ADM cycle.

Based on TOGAF® 9, which of the following answers best addresses this requirement?

ANSWERS

A. In the Preliminary Phase, identify the stakeholders that will assist in the development of the architecture to which the enterprise will be partitioned. In Phase A, identify the proper transition phases for migration. In Phases B-D, conduct several iterations of architecture development and produce the Architecture Vision. In Phase E, after completing the development of all aspects of the solution, produce a detailed Implementation and Migration plan.

B. In the Preliminary Phase, agree to a set of architecture principles with the stakeholders; analyze current governance and support frameworks, and identify any changes needed for this transition; gather a team of competent individuals to undergo TOGAF® training. In Phase A, tailor TOGAF® for the project; identify the main, secondary, and tertiary enterprises affected by this transition; produce a Statement of Architecture Work document.

C. In the Preliminary Phase, agree to a set of architecture principles with the stakeholders; analyze current governance and support frameworks, establish a set of principles to guide the development of the transition; assess the ability of the enterprise to undergo change; conduct a business value assessment to establish work packages and order of transition phases. In Phases B-D, create an architecture with an emphasis on data integrity, technology interoperability and reporting capabilities.

D. In the Preliminary Phase, you must confirm with the stakeholders what governance and support frameworks are in use and agree to modifications that may be needed in the development of the solution; next, you have the stakeholders recommend a team of competent individuals to undergo TOGAF® training so they will understand how to execute the transitions to be made; follow this by establishing the architecture principles needed and begin adaptation of TOGAF® for this project; then produce a Request for Architecture Work document.

SCENARIO #8 JDKP Pharmaceuticals

BACKGROUND

JDKP currently has initiatives under way to improve its data sharing with internal and external partners, including adoption of an enterprise-wide standard for formatting data and several projects aimed at enhancing its ability to share data. Effective data sharing is essential to its review and approval process, inspection of imports and manufacturing facilities, and tracking of contaminated products. However, these projects have made mixed progress, and significant work remains for JDKP to fully implement standardized data sharing. Further, JDKP has not comprehensively assessed information-sharing needs to ensure that its systems and databases are organized for effective information sharing. This is needed to help ensure more efficient access to and sharing of key information supporting its mission.

The CIO and relevant stakeholders have reached consensus on the strategy for beginning the modernization of the IT infrastructure by implementing an optimal data sharing solution involving the stratification of data collection, storage, and dissemination. They want a logically centralized, physically distributed data system to be designed and implemented with a flawless integration with other technologies and applications under re-evaluation for modernization.

The stakeholders have reservations about the risks inherent in migrating legacy data into the new system. Concerns of data loss and data corruption are issues that provided an initial rejection of a few of the stakeholders. The CIO presented a plan for development of the new data structure: it will be divided into two parts: 1) discovery of current data usage and 2) the target data structure. The stakeholders would have complete transparency to the planning, there would be weekly reviews, and that any of the stakeholders would have the power to put a hold on the planning at the conclusion of those reviews.

QUESTION

Refer to the scenario

As Chief Architect, you have directed the Lead Architect to identify the relevant viewpoints in the Architecture Development baseline iteration. Which of the below would represent the best approach? Based on TOGAF® 9, which of the following is the best answer?

ANSWERS

A. In Phase B, generate an Organization/Actor Catalog, a Business Interaction Matrix, and a Business Service/Information Catalog. In Phase C, Data Architecture, generate a System/Data Matrix, a Class Diagram, and a Class Hierarchy Diagram. In Phase C, Application Architecture, create an Application Portfolio Catalog and an Application Communication Diagram. In Phase D, produce a System/Technology Matrix.

B. Phases B and D are not necessary since this is only about the data architecture. In Phase C, Data Architecture, generate all of the artifacts. There is no need for an iteration of Phase C, Application Architecture since the stakeholders are only concerned about data.

C. In Phase B, generate a Driver/Goal/Objective Catalog, a Business Interaction Matrix, and a Business Use-Case Diagram. In Phase C, Data Architecture, generate a Data Entity/Data Component Catalog, a Data Entity/Business Function Matrix, a System/Data Matrix, and a Data Dissemination Diagram. In Phase C, Application Architecture, create an Application Portfolio Catalog, an Interface Catalog, a System/Function Matrix, and an Application Communication Diagram. In Phase D, produce a Technology Portfolio Catalog, and a System/Technology Matrix.

D. In Phase B, generate an Organization/Actor Catalog, a Role Catalog, a Location Catalog, and a Process/Event/Control/Product Catalog, a Functional Decomposition Diagram, and an Organization Decomposition Diagram. In Phase C, Data Architecture, generate all of the Catalogs, Matrices, and Core Diagrams, plus the Data Migration Diagram.

SCENARIO SET #1 ANSWER KEYS

SCENARIO 1 Visum Futurum ST, Inc.

Topic		ADM Phases: Architecture Development (Phases B, C, D)
Subjects/Rationale		Artifacts: The student must be able to select the appropriate artifacts for the Architecture Development cycle to address stakeholder concerns.
Most Correct	A	All of the artifacts in this answer address the concerns of the executives and stakeholders.
Second Best	C	While this may seem identical to answer A, it is misleading because it implies that all of the artifacts listed for Phases B-C are used across the Architectures when they are supposed to be specific to the Phase.
Third Best	D	This answer has fewer correct artifacts, for example, the Process/Event/Control/Product Catalog is a better fit for the target architecture.
Distractor	B	Many of the viewpoints do not exist in the TOGAF® model.

SCENARIO #2 SoCal Bank

Topic		Architecture Content Framework: Metamodel Extensions
Subjects/Rationale		This scenario addresses identification of the appropriate extensions to the content metamodel to address stakeholder concerns.
Most Correct	B	The scenario calls for extensions in the Governance, Services, and Motivation Metamodels
Second Best	C	Process Modeling does not apply; it is concerned with stateful architectural requirements
Third Best	D	There is no mention of data issues in the list of concerns
Distractor	A	None of the listed extensions is applicable

SCENARIO #3 Pyramid Sales

Topic		ADM: Phase E: Opportunities and Solutions
Subjects/Rationale		The student should understand the tasks associated with the first phase that begins development of the actual solution.
Most Correct	C	All of these elements are found in the Steps section for Phase E
Second Best	B	Not all of the elements needed are shown; Phase E output does not include the Final Architecture Roadmap and Implementation and Migration Plan.
Third Best	D	This answer wanders through the ADM; is not focused enough to realize the solution.
Distractor	A	Instructions did not include the Chief Architect's latitude to change the sequencing of the mobile during a second phase.

SCENARIO #4 Portable Foundations

Topic		Content Metamodel Extensions
Subjects/Rationale		This scenario asks for the identification of the correct application of Content Metamodel extensions.
Most Correct	B	This answer provides the correct answer since it identifies the content metamodel extensions for compliance with regulatory requirements (Process Modeling Extensions) as well as dealing with rationalization of infrastructure elements (Infrastructure Consolidation Extensions).
Second Best	D	Does not include Process Modeling extension, which is needed for addressing regulatory constraints.
Third Best	A	While these may be tasks performed in the Architecture Development Iteration, they do not directly address stakeholder concerns.
Distractor	C	This is not specifically a Risk Management scenario.

SCENARIO #5 Phoenix Motor Oil (PMOL)

Topic		The ADM Phases: Governance (Phase G)
Subjects/Rationale		This question addresses the importance of and methods by which the Implementation Team controls the implementation and assures the major stakeholders of continual compliance to the Implementation Plan.
Most Correct	A	This is the best answer. It provides a logical plan from beginning to end of each transition phase. It also addresses the concerns of cost overruns by allowing the Architecture Board to approve changes before they occur; they will be able to assess risks and understand better why costs increase if they are unavoidable.
Second Best	C	While most of the elements involved with Phase G are listed, this answer does not address the Architecture Board's concern with budgetary constraints.
Third Best	B	Some of the first elements of this answer are acceptable, but the AB does not run the compliance review, that is done by the Lead Architect. Also, if the AB only gets a summary of changes after the fact, they will not have a say in financial increases to the project.
Distractor	D	This is a recipe for disaster. By switching out teams in the hopes of cross-training and forcing transparency, this solution would bring about confusion among the members of the EA team.

SCENARIO #6 eFortitude

Topic		Risk Management
Subjects/Rationale		The student should know the steps for Risk Management and when in the ADM they occur.
Most Correct	B	Provides the complete answers as presented in TOGAF®.
Second Best	C	Moves most of the Risk Management steps into the Architecture Development Iteration. Risk mitigation is determined in Phase A.
Third Best	A	The right steps in the wrong Phases
Distractor	D	A jumble of incorrect steps in the wrong Phases.

SCENARIO #7 Government Accounting Agency (GAO)

Topic		Preliminary Phase
Subjects/Rationale		Scenario focuses on steps in the Preliminary Phase
Most Correct	D	Answer A addresses the focus of the task assigned to the Chief Architect, that of establishing the enterprise architecture team and preparing for execution of the ADM cycle, which all occurs in the Preliminary Phase.
Second Best	B	While establishing a set of architecture principles is correct, it is usually accomplished by the enterprise architecture team, which has not yet been identified and trained. All of the activities that satisfy the constraints of the task given to the Chief Architect occur in the Preliminary Phase.
Third Best	C	All of the tasks identified in this answer may be appropriate later in solution development, but the charter for now is just to establish TOGAF® as the framework.
Distractor	A	This answer is completely wrong.

SCENARIO #8 JDKP Pharmaceuticals

Topic		Baseline iteration of Phases B-D
Subjects/Rationale		The scenario emphasizes the use of artifacts during Architecture Development Iteration.
Most Correct	C	Answer C provides all of the necessary elements to address getting a full understanding of the current usage of data between applications and business functions and organizations, to prepare a gap analysis for rationalizing data duplication, and establishing a baseline of the current visibility of data across the enterprise.
Second Best	A	Answer A has many of the proper artifacts, but does not produce a full understanding of data elements, which would be provided in such artifacts as the Driver/Goal/Objective Catalog and Data Entity/Business Function Matrix.
Third Best	D	Answer D is out of focus and would not produce relevant information to proceed to the target iteration.
Distractor	B	Answer B is wrong since development of the Data Architecture alone, without an understanding of how data is used, shared, controlled, and served.

Set 2: Scenarios 9 - 16

SCENARIO #9 Jetstream Hydrocycles #1

BACKGROUND

Jetstream Hydrocycles (JHC) is a manufacturer of high-speed personal watercrafts (PWC). They have only been in the business three years, but are one of the top sellers of PWCs in the country. They are the first PWC manufacturer to produce dual-propeller water vehicles, which led the industry to adopt similar configurations. One of their competitors, PowerWave, was testing their first dual-prop prototype when they suddenly went bankrupt. JHC offered to buy them out at 50 cents on the dollar. . This took a major hit on the bottom line, but the board of directors supported the executives to proceed. They felt that JHC could greatly increase their market share by this acquisition. Also, because PowerWave had an existing R&D center, they believe it could be leveraged to accelerate the new products to market.

JHC will now have to merge the assets from PowerWave into their enterprise. Because the architecture of the two corporations is so diverse, they know that it will take much due diligence to make a smooth migration. They also are considering not assimilating the acquisition into JHC, but establishing a new architecture that would reduce efforts to "shoe-horn in" the new with the old. This is a risky move, but they also retained the PowerWave enterprise architecture team who had experience with these kinds of transitions.

The executive leadership has scheduled a meeting to inform the Chief Architect of the proposed plan. They want to know if their vision makes sense, if it is doable, if they have the right people and tools, and what impact they can expect to the various business units would be.

QUESTION

Refer to the scenario

Your role is the Chief Architect

Based on TOGAF® 9, which of the following is the best answer?

ANSWERS

A. Determine the business units that will be involved with the transition and to what degree each will be impacted. Confirm how Jetstream provided governance and established support frameworks. Conduct an enterprise architecture change maturity assessment and define requests for change to existing business programs and projects. Discover the constraints on the architecture work; assess budget requirements. Establish the architecture principles around which architecture governance will be founded. Tailor terminology, process, and content from TOGAF® to meet the requirements of the new architecture. Implement architecture tools.

B. Determine the business units that will be involved with the transition and to what degree each will be impacted. Confirm how Jetstream provided governance and established support frameworks. Conduct a Risk Impact Assessment and a Business Transition Readiness Assessment. Discover the constraints on the architecture work; assess budget requirements. Establish the architecture principles around which architecture governance will be founded. Tailor terminology, process, and content from TOGAF® to meet the requirements of the new architecture. Implement architecture tools.

C. Identify stakeholders, concerns, and business requirements. Confirm how Jetstream provided governance and established support frameworks. Confirm and elaborate business goals, business drivers, and constraints. Conduct a Risk Impact Assessment and a Business Transition Readiness Assessment. Discover the constraints on the architecture work; assess budget requirements. Establish the architecture principles around which architecture governance will be founded. Tailor terminology, process, and content from TOGAF® to meet the requirements of the new architecture. Implement architecture tools.

D. Identify changed requirements and ensure the requirements are prioritized by the architect(s) responsible for the current phase, and by the relevant stakeholders. Record new priorities. Ensure that any conflicts are identified and managed through the phases to a successful conclusion and prioritization. Record requirements priorities and place in the Requirements Repository. Generate a Requirements Impact Statement for steering the architecture team. Update the Requirements Repository with information relating to the changes requested, including stakeholder views affected.

SCENARIO #10 Jetstream Hydrocycles #2

BACKGROUND

Jetstream HydroCycles (JHC) is a manufacturer of high-speed personal watercrafts (PWC). They have only been in the business three years, but are one of the top sellers of PWCs in the country. They are the first PWC manufacturer to produce dual-propeller water vehicles, which led the industry to adopt similar configurations. One of their competitors, PowerWave, was testing their first dual-prop prototype when they suddenly went bankrupt. JHC offered to buy them out at 50 cents on the dollar. This took a major hit on the bottom line, but the board of directors supported the executives to proceed. They felt that JHC could greatly increase their market share by this acquisition. Also, because PowerWave had an existing R&D center, they believe it could be leveraged to accelerate the new products to market.

JHC will now have to merge the assets from PowerWave into their enterprise. Because the architecture of the two corporations is so diverse, they know that it will take much due diligence to make a smooth migration. They also are considering not assimilating the acquisition into JHC, but establishing a new architecture that would reduce efforts to "shoe-horn in" the new with the old. This is a risky move, but they also retained the PowerWave enterprise architecture team who had experience with these kinds of transitions.

The new vision has been approved, the governance and support frameworks are in place, architecture principles have been enumerated, TOGAF® has been adapted and the EA team has implanted architecture tools. The stakeholders have reviewed the Request for Architecture Work, so the ADM cycle is about to begin. The major concern of the stakeholders—and executives—is whether or not JHC is fully prepared to execute the program. Since both JHC and PowerWave will be moving to a divergent architecture, they want to make sure the Vision is understood and that readiness factors have been diligently examined.

QUESTION

Refer to the scenario

Your role is the Business Architect.

The time has come to conduct the Business Transformation Readiness Assessment. The Lead Architect has asked you to assess the readiness factors of the enterprise to embark on the transition.

Based on TOGAF® 9, which of the following is the best answer?

ANSWERS

A. Establish the architecture project; identify stakeholders, concerns, and business requirements; confirm and elaborate business goals, business drivers, and constraints; evaluate business capabilities; assess readiness for business transformation; assess the baseline architecture from which to examine the current readiness; confirm and elaborate Architecture Principles, including business principles; develop Architecture Vision; define the Target Architecture value propositions and KPIs; identify the business transformation risks and mitigation activities; define the scope and issue a Statement of Architecture Work.

B. First, assess the baseline architecture from which to examine the current readiness. Next, proceed through the Architecture Development cycle and in Phase E, finalize the gaps found in Phases B-D. last, build a matrix that evaluates readiness factors according to 1) the urgency that a factor be implemented in respect to other factors; 2) the status of the factor's readiness from a low state—meaning that there is much pre-work to perform before implementation—to a high state where there are no further dependencies and can proceed; 3) the degree of difficulty to fix an issue with a factor that has to be overcome.

C. First, assess vision readiness in view of the target established for the enterprise. Next, build a matrix that evaluates readiness factors according to 1) the urgency that a factor be implemented in respect to other factors; 2) the status of the factor's readiness from a low state—meaning that there is much pre-work to perform before implementation—to a high state where there are no further dependencies and can proceed; 3) the degree of difficulty to fix an issue with a factor that has to be overcome. Last, establish a series of actions to enable the factors to change to a favorable state.

D. First, assess vision readiness in view of where the enterprise is and of where the enterprise needs to be. Next, build a matrix that evaluates readiness factors according to 1) the urgency that a factor be implemented in respect to other factors; 2) the status of the factor's readiness from a low state—meaning that there is much pre-work to perform before implementation—to a high state where there are no further dependencies and can proceed; 3) the degree of difficulty to fix an issue with a factor that has to be overcome. Last, establish a series of actions to enable the factors to change to a favorable state.

SCENARIO #11 Jetstream Hydrocycles #3

BACKGROUND

Jetstream Hydrocycles (JHC) is a manufacturer of high-speed personal watercrafts (PWC). They have only been in the business three years, but are one of the top sellers of PWCs in the country. They are the first PWC manufacturer to produce dual-propeller water vehicles, which led the industry to adopt similar configurations. One of their competitors, PowerWave, was testing their first dual-prop prototype when they suddenly went bankrupt. JHC offered to buy them out at 50 cents on the dollar. This took a major hit on the bottom line, but the board of directors supported the executives to proceed. They felt that JHC could greatly increase their market share by this acquisition. Also, because PowerWave had an existing R&D center, they believe it could be leveraged to accelerate the new products to market.

JHC will now have to merge the assets from PowerWave into their enterprise. Because the architecture of the two corporations is so diverse, they know that it will take much due diligence to make a smooth migration. They also are considering not assimilating the acquisition into JHC, but establishing a new architecture that would reduce efforts to "shoe-horn in" the new with the old. This is a risky move, but they also retained the PowerWave enterprise architecture team who had experience with these kinds of transitions.

After several cycles of the Architecture Capability Iteration, the stakeholders have signed off on the Request for Architecture Work, Architecture Vision, and Statement of Architecture Work. The EA team is now prepared to carry the program through the Architecture Development Iteration. Because of the apparent differences between the two enterprises, the EA team will be taking considerable care in documenting all of the gaps that will be found.

QUESTION

Refer to the scenario

Your role is the Lead Architect. You will now lead your team through the Architecture Development Cycle.

Based on TOGAF® 9, which of the following is the best answer?

ANSWERS

A. In the first iteration of the Architecture Development iteration, for phases B-D, in each phase, select reference models, viewpoints, and tools; develop baseline architecture description; in the second iteration, develop the target architecture. Document the gaps between the two architectures; define candidate roadmap components; resolve impacts across the Architecture Landscape; conduct formal stakeholder review; and finalize the architecture. In Phase E, create a gap analysis matrix filling the baseline axis with the services in place in both of the enterprises' architecture. Document the gaps between the two architectures.

B. In the first iteration of the Architecture Development iteration, for phases B-D, in each phase, select reference models, viewpoints, and tools; develop baseline architecture description; create a gap analysis matrix filling the baseline axis with the services in place in both of the enterprises' architecture. In the second iteration, develop the target architecture and enumerate the gap analysis matrix with the target services listed along the target services axis. Document the gaps between the two architectures; define candidate roadmap components; resolve impacts across the Architecture Landscape; conduct formal stakeholder review; and finalize the architecture.

C. In the first iteration of the Architecture Development iteration, for phases A-D, in each phase, select reference views; develop baseline architecture description; in the second iteration, develop the target architecture. In Phase E, finalize the Implementation and Development Plan; define candidate roadmap components; resolve impacts across the Architecture Landscape; conduct formal stakeholder review. In Phase F, begin the implementation after setting up an Architecture Review Board and Change Control Board.

D. In the first iteration of the Architecture Development iteration, for phases B-D, in each phase, select reference models, viewpoints, and tools; develop baseline and target architecture descriptions. Define candidate roadmap components; resolve impacts across the Architecture Landscape; conduct formal stakeholder review; and finalize the architecture; and produce the refined Architecture Vision, Data Entity/Data Component Catalog, Data Entity/Business Function Matrix, Data Migration Diagram; and the Architecture Roadmap.

SCENARIO #12 Jetstream Hydrocycles #4

BACKGROUND

Jetstream Hydrocycles (JHC) is a manufacturer of high-speed personal watercrafts (PWC). They have only been in the business three years, but are one of the top sellers of PWCs in the country. They are the first PWC manufacturer to produce dual-propeller water vehicles, which led the industry to adopt similar configurations. One of their competitors, PowerWave, was testing their first dual-prop prototype when they suddenly went bankrupt. JHC offered to buy them out at 50 cents on the dollar. This took a major hit on the bottom line, but the board of directors supported the executives to proceed. They felt that JHC could greatly increase their market share by this acquisition. Also, because PowerWave had an existing R&D center, they believe it could be leveraged to accelerate the new products to market.

JHC will now have to merge the assets from PowerWave into their enterprise. Because the architecture of the two corporations is so diverse, they know that it will take much due diligence to make a smooth migration. They also are considering not assimilating the acquisition into JHC, but establishing a new architecture that would reduce efforts to "shoe-horn in" the new with the old. This is a risky move, but they also retained the PowerWave enterprise architecture team who had experience with these kinds of transitions.

The EA team has now completed the Architecture Development Iteration and will now begin the process of establishing how to deliver the architecture. The concern of the stakeholders and executives is the smoothest possible migration and are keen to understand all the steps that will be taken to ensure this. Before the actual implementation and migration plan is created, they want the draft version to be presented at the next quarterly program meeting.

QUESTION

Refer to the scenario

Your role is the Solutions Architect.

The Chief Architect has handed over to you the documentation output from the Architecture Development Iteration and assigned you the task to produce the draft Implementation and Migration Plan. Based on TOGAF® 9, which of the following is the best answer?

ANSWERS

A. Conduct a performance evaluation, establish CSFs and MOEs to allow capability managers to approve and monitor the progress of the architecture transformation. Get an understanding of the ROI of the transformation output. Make sure there is a business value assigned to each sub-project. Understand the strategic fit of the implementation plans and use work products to create SBBs and ABBs by pulling from the Enterprise Continuum and Architecture

Repository. Use a cost/benefit analysis and risk validation to prioritize the migration projects. Formally review the risk assessment and revise it as necessary ensuring that there is a full understanding of the residual risk associated with the prioritization and the projected funding line.

B. Coordinate business planning, enterprise architecture, portfolio/project management, and operations management frameworks. Identify SBBs that could potentially address one or more gaps and their associated ABBs. Rationalize the gaps found in the Consolidated Gaps, Solutions, and Dependencies Matrix. Establish the best direction for creating an efficient and effective target architecture addressing all of the business functions. Minimize interoperability conflicts by closely reviewing re-used building blocks, COTS products and third party services. Refine and validate dependencies, confirm the readiness and risks for business transformation; formulate the draft implementation and migration strategy. Assign a business value to each work package. Finally, create the Architecture Roadmap and mid-level Implementation and Migration Plan.

C. Identify SBBs that could potentially address one or more gaps and their associated ABBs. Rationalize the gaps found in the Consolidated Gaps, Solutions, and Dependencies Matrix. Establish the best direction for creating an efficient and effective target architecture addressing all of the business functions. Minimize interoperability conflicts by closely reviewing re-used building blocks, COTS products and third party services. Refine and validate dependencies, confirm the readiness and risks for business transformation; formulate the draft implementation and migration strategy. Group the major work packages for creating the smoothest transition from baseline to target architectures. Determine the transition architectures. Finally, create the Architecture Roadmap and low-level Implementation and Migration Plan.

D. Identify SBBs that could potentially address one or more gaps and their associated ABBs. Rationalize the gaps found in the Consolidated Gaps, Solutions, and Dependencies Matrix. Establish the best direction for creating an efficient and effective target architecture addressing all of the business functions. Minimize interoperability conflicts by closely reviewing re-used building blocks, COTS products and third party services. Refine and validate dependencies, confirm the readiness and risks for business transformation; formulate the draft implementation and migration strategy. Group the major work packages for creating the smoothest transition from baseline to target architectures. Determine the transition architectures. Finally, create the Architecture Roadmap and high-level Implementation and Migration Plan.

SCENARIO #13 Jetstream Hydrocycles #5

BACKGROUND

Jetstream Hydrocycles (JHC) is a manufacturer of high-speed personal watercrafts (PWC). They have only been in the business three years, but are one of the top sellers of PWCs in the country. They are the first PWC manufacturer to produce dual-propeller water vehicles, which led the industry to adopt similar configurations. One of their competitors, PowerWave, was testing their first dual-prop prototype when they suddenly went bankrupt. JHC offered to buy them out at 50 cents on the dollar. . This took a major hit on the bottom line, but the board of directors supported the executives to proceed. They felt that JHC could greatly increase their market share by this acquisition. Also, because PowerWave had an existing R&D center, they believe it could be leveraged to accelerate the new products to market.

JHC will now have to merge the assets from PowerWave into their enterprise. Because the architecture of the two corporations is so diverse, they know that it will take much due diligence to make a smooth migration. They also are considering not assimilating the acquisition into JHC, but establishing a new architecture that would reduce efforts to "shoe-horn in" the new with the old. This is a risky move, but they also retained the PowerWave enterprise architecture team who had experience with these kinds of transitions.

The plan was approved and the EA team was chartered to conduct the ADM Cycle to implement the program. The Architecture Development Iteration is complete and the team is now in the Transition Planning Iteration. Over the course of the ADM Cycle, the stakeholders have approved each Phase but have grown more anxious about the actual implementation now that they have seen the depth of complexity and risks that approach. The EA team has completed Phase E and is now moving into the last phase before implementation begins. The stakeholders have addressed their concerns to the Chief Architect.

QUESTION

Refer to the scenario

Your role is Solution Architect

The Chief Architect has asked you to prepare the implementation of the architecture.

Based on TOGAF® 9, which of the following is the best answer?

ANSWERS

A. Coordinate the interaction of the frameworks of business planning, enterprise architecture, portfolio/project management, and operations management. Distinguish the value of each work package based on performance, ROI, Requests for Information, and Multiple Organization Enterprises. Make sure there is a strategic fit. Ensure that resources, time and method of delivery are available. Prioritize the separate projects using a business transformation readiness assessment and risk validation. Review and confirm the Architecture Roadmap and Architecture Definition Document. Generate the draft Implementation and Migration Plan.

B. Coordinate the interaction of the frameworks of business planning, enterprise architecture, portfolio/project management, and operations management. Distinguish the value of each work package based on performance, ROI, CSFs, and MOE. Make sure there is a strategic fit. Make sure that resources, time and method of delivery are available. Prioritize the separate projects using a cost/benefit assessment and risk validation. Review and confirm the Architecture Roadmap and Architecture Definition Document. Generate the finalized Implementation and Migration Plan.

C. Finalize the Business, Data, Application, and Technology Architecture Documents. Build ABBs from suitable SBBs from the Enterprise Continuum. Select the architecture team that will conduct the operational tasks for migration. Distinguish the value of each work package based on performance, ROI, CSFs, and MOE. Prioritize the separate projects using a cost/benefit assessment and risk validation. Review and confirm the Architecture Roadmap and Architecture Definition Document. Generate the draft Implementation and Migration Plan. Update the Architecture Vision.

D. Review the finalized Implementation Plan from Phase E. Evaluate the ROI, CSFs, and MOE are in line with the Architecture Vision. Drive the cost/benefit analysis through completion to prioritize the work packages. Make sure there is a strategic fit. Make sure all resources, time, and availability of delivery vehicles are in place. Create the final drafts of the Architecture Definition Document, Architecture Requirements Specification, and Architecture Roadmap. Place re-usable artifacts into the Architecture Repository, publish version 1.1 of the Implementation and Migration Plan.

SCENARIO #14 Jetstream Hydrocycles #6

BACKGROUND

Jetstream Hydrocycles (JHC) is a manufacturer of high-speed personal watercrafts (PWC). They have only been in the business three years, but are one of the top sellers of PWCs in the country. They are the first PWC manufacturer to produce dual-propeller water vehicles, which led the industry to adopt similar configurations. One of their competitors, PowerWave, was testing their first dual-prop prototype when they suddenly went bankrupt. JHC offered to buy them out at 50 cents on the dollar. This took a major hit on the bottom line, but the board of directors supported the executives to proceed. They felt that JHC could greatly increase their market share by this acquisition. Also, because PowerWave had an existing R&D center, they believe it could be leveraged to accelerate the new products to market.

JHC will now have to merge the assets from PowerWave into their enterprise. Because the architecture of the two corporations is so diverse, they know that it will take much due diligence to make a smooth migration. They also are considering not assimilating the acquisition into JHC, but establishing a new architecture that would reduce efforts to "shoe-horn in" the new with the old. This is a risky move, but they also retained the PowerWave enterprise architecture team who had experience with these kinds of transitions.

The EA team has completed the Architecture Development Iteration and Transition and Planning Iteration and is now about to begin the Architecture Governance Implementation. At this time, the Architecture Review Board determined that two of the eight major shareholders had exhibited undue influence on the development of the solution, which would result in an imbalance of priorities in their favor. Not only that, but the resulting framework, if implemented, would have fatal flaws corrupting the final architecture.

QUESTION

Refer to the scenario

Your role is the Chief Architect and the Architecture Board has asked you to address and fix this issue. The project has been halted until the appropriate changes have been made, so timely success is paramount. Which of the answers below describes the best actions to take, in the right order, to re-align the Architecture Roadmap?

Based on TOGAF® 9, which of the following is the best answer?

ANSWERS

A. Create a Requirements Impact Assessment. Identify the stakeholder priority of the requirements to date. Identify the phases that will have to be revisited due to the problem at hand. Confirm governance and support frameworks. Add an architecture principle: Responsibility: Each contracted party is required to act responsibly to the organization and its stakeholders. Update the Architecture Roadmap. Update the Requirements Impact Assessment. Re-evaluate and adjust, as necessary, the architecture design through another iteration of the Architecture Development Iteration. Update governance models and frameworks.

B. Identify the stakeholder priority of the requirements to date. Identify the phases that will have to be revisited due to the problem at hand. Create a Requirements Impact Assessment. Add an architecture principle: Fairness: All decisions taken, processes used, and their implementation will not be allowed to create unfair advantage to any one particular party. Confirm governance and support frameworks. Produce a new stakeholder map. Publish the Architecture Vision. Re-evaluate and adjust, as necessary, the architecture design through another iteration of the Architecture Development Iteration. Update governance models and frameworks. Update the Architecture Roadmap.

C. Identify the stakeholder priority of the requirements to date. Identify the phases that will have to be revisited due to the problem at hand. Create a Requirements Impact Assessment. Redefine and reorganize the enterprise architecture team. Produce a new stakeholder map. Re-evaluate and adjust, as necessary, gaps in the architecture design through another iteration of the Architecture Development Iteration. Update governance models and frameworks. Determine business constraints for implementation. Update the Architecture Roadmap.

D. Create a new Architecture Vision. Update the Implementation and Migration Plan. Discover and fill gaps during a reiteration of the Implementation and Migration Plan. Form the Architecture Governance Board to true industry standards. Create a Requirements Impact Assessment. Redefine and reorganize the enterprise architecture team. Produce a new stakeholder map. Re-evaluate and adjust, as necessary, the architecture design through another iteration of the Architecture Development Iteration. Update governance models and frameworks.

SCENARIO #15 Jetstream Hydrocycles #7

BACKGROUND

Jetstream Hydrocycles (JHC) is a manufacturer of high-speed personal watercrafts (PWC). They have only been in the business three years, but are one of the top sellers of PWCs in the country. They are the first PWC manufacturer to produce dual-propeller water vehicles, which led the industry to adopt similar configurations. One of their competitors, PowerWave, was testing their first dual-prop prototype when they suddenly went bankrupt. JHC offered to buy them out at 50 cents on the dollar. . This took a major hit on the bottom line, but the board of directors supported the executives to proceed. They felt that JHC could greatly increase their market share by this acquisition. Also, because PowerWave had an existing R&D center, they believe it could be leveraged to accelerate the new products to market.

JHC will now have to merge the assets from PowerWave into their enterprise. Because the architecture of the two corporations is so diverse, they know that it will take much due diligence to make a smooth migration. They also are considering not assimilating the acquisition into JHC, but establishing a new architecture that would reduce efforts to "shoe-horn in" the new with the old. This is a risky move, but they also retained the PowerWave enterprise architecture team who had experience with these kinds of transitions.

JHC has been successfully conducting its migration to the new homogenized architecture, having to perform some additional iterations of the ADM due to some further discoveries of internal issues and unforeseen risks during migration. Two new impacts have come from exterior risks. One is the result of the Research and Development team successfully developing a more efficient and less-costly manufacturing platform which will decrease costs and time-to-market. The other is a change in government regulations to further reduce exhaust emissions by 3.5% within the next 2 years.

QUESTION

Refer to the scenario

Your role is the Solutions Architect. The Chief Architect has asked you to reassess business, data, application, and technology changes necessary to meet these challenges.

Based on TOGAF® 9, which of the following is the best answer?

ANSWERS

A. Begin with the Business Architecture Phase, identify gaps in the current business architecture to meet the new requirements; update the Organization/Actor Catalog, Driver/Goal/Objective Catalog, the Business Service/Function Catalog, Location Catalog, Contract/Measure Catalog, and Business Interaction Matrix. Since the new elements of the architecture are not indicative of changes to the Information Systems Architecture, a pass through Phase C is not necessary. In the Technology Phase, identify gaps in the current technology infrastructure to meet the demands of new manufacturing constraints; then update the Technology Portfolio Catalog, the Application/Technology Matrix, Platform Description Diagram, and Network Computing Hardware Diagram to document additions and changes to fill the gaps in the Technology Architecture. In Phase E, consolidate the gaps from phases A-D. Update the Communications Engineering Diagram, the Project Context Diagram, and Benefits Diagram; in the Requirements Catalog, restate the Requirements, Assumptions, Constraints, and Gaps to coincide with the updated technologies.

B. Restart the Architecture Capability Iteration and produce a new Request for Architecture Work for Phase A. In Phase A, establish a new architecture project, identify stakeholder concerns, evaluate business capabilities, and assess business transformation readiness assessments for the updated architecture. Create a new set of Architecture Principles, KPIs, and CMM. Modify the Business, Data, Application, and Technology Architectures to adhere to the new solution. Conduct the Transition Planning Iteration to prepare for implementation and hand off the new solution to the Architecture Review Board for final analysis.

C. Begin with the Technology Phase and identify gaps in the current technology infrastructure to meet the demands of new manufacturing constraints; then update the Technology Portfolio Catalog, the Application/Technology Matrix, Platform Description Diagram, and Network Computing Hardware Diagram to document additions and changes to fill the gaps in the Technology Architecture. Follow this with a pass through the Application Architecture with a gap analysis to determine any deficiencies in the applications to perform possible new functions; update the Application Portfolio, Interface Catalog, Application Interaction Matrix, and Application Use-Case Diagram. Then perform an iteration of the Data Architecture, first identifying possible gaps in the current design to fulfill the needs of the new architecture; update the Application/Data Matrix, and the Logical Data Diagram as needed. Last, execute an iteration of the Business Architecture, first conducting a gap analysis to see what business processes will be affected; update the Business Service/Function Catalog, the Process/Event/Control/Product Catalog, the Functional Decomposition Diagram, the Product Lifecycle Diagram, and the Goal/Objective/Service Diagram.

D. Begin with the Technology Phase and identify gaps in the current technology infrastructure to meet the demands of new manufacturing constraints; then update the Technology Portfolio Catalog, the Application/Technology Matrix, Platform Description Diagram, and Network Computing Hardware Diagram to document additions and changes to fill the gaps in the Technology Architecture.

Follow this with a pass through the Application Architecture with a gap analysis to determine any deficiencies in the applications to perform possible new functions; update the Application Portfolio, Application/Data Matrix, Application Interaction Matrix, Logical Data Diagram, and Application Use-Case Diagram. Then perform an iteration of the Data Architecture, first identifying possible gaps in the current design to fulfill the needs of the new architecture; update the Interface Catalog, and the Logical Data Diagram as needed. Last, execute an iteration of the Business Architecture, first conducting a gap analysis to see what business processes will be affected; update the Business Service/Function Catalog, the Process/Event/Control/Product Catalog, the Functional Decomposition Diagram, the Product Lifecycle Diagram, and the Goal/Objective/Service Diagram.

SCENARIO #16 Jetstream Hydrocycles #8

BACKGROUND

Jetstream Hydrocycles (JHC) is a manufacturer of high-speed personal watercrafts (PWC). They have only been in the business three years, but are one of the top sellers of PWCs in the country. They are the first PWC manufacturer to produce dual-propeller water vehicles, which led the industry to adopt similar configurations. One of their competitors, PowerWave, was testing their first dual-prop prototype when they suddenly went bankrupt. JHC offered to buy them out at 50 cents on the dollar. This took a major hit on the bottom line, but the board of directors supported the executives to proceed. They felt that JHC could greatly increase their market share by this acquisition. Also, because PowerWave had an existing R&D center, they believe it could be leveraged to accelerate the new products to market.

JHC will now have to merge the assets from PowerWave into their enterprise. Because the architecture of the two corporations is so diverse, they know that it will take much due diligence to make a smooth migration. They also are considering not assimilating the acquisition into JHC, but establishing a new architecture that would reduce efforts to "shoe-horn in" the new with the old. This is a risky move, but they also retained the PowerWave enterprise architecture team who had experience with these kinds of transitions.

The major stakeholders and executives were very concerned about duplicative resources across the two enterprises. They wanted to make sure that these resources could be rationalized during the transition. Manufacturing, R&D, administrative staff, sales force, applications, databases, and locations were all elements of concern. They firmly stipulated that the new architecture address this concern and wanted an assurance of compliance from the Chief Architect that the EA team would do so.

QUESTION

Refer to the scenario

Your role is the Chief Architect. The stakeholders have asked you to iterate your plan to alleviate their concerns in this matter.

Based on TOGAF® 9, which of the following best addresses these concerns?

ANSWERS

A. During the Architecture Vision Phase, the EA team will include these extensions in the high-level Information Systems Architecture: an entity identifying the location of the IT assets; application abstractions to define application capability over actual applications; abstract product types. They will also create the templates for the Data Entity/Business Function Matrix, Logical Data Diagram, Data Dissemination Diagram, Application Portfolio Catalog,

Application/Organization Matrix, Application/Function Matrix, Application Communication Diagram, and Application and User Location Diagram.

B. During the Information Systems Architecture Phase, the EA team will include these extensions in the high-level Information Systems Architecture: an entity identifying the location of the IT assets; application abstractions to define application capability over actual applications; abstract product types. They will also create the templates for the Data Entity/Business Function Matrix, Logical Data Diagram, Data Dissemination Diagram, Application Portfolio Catalog, Application/Organization Matrix, Application/Function Matrix, Application Communication Diagram, and Application and User Location Diagram.

C. During the Architecture Vision Phase, the EA team will include these extensions in the high-level Information Systems Architecture: an IS service as an extension of business service; create products to represent the output of a process; application abstractions to define application capability over actual applications; and create physical data components that implement logical data components that are analogous to databases, registries, repositories, schemas, and other techniques of segmenting data.

D. During Phase D, the EA team will extend the high-level Information Systems Architecture with: an entity identifying the location of the manufacturing facilities; human resource abstractions to define human resource capability over actual capability; abstract production types. They will also create the templates for the Data Entity Catalog, Physical Data Matrix, Data Directive Diagram, Application Portfolio Diagram, Application/Organization/Business Function Matrix, Application/Function/Actor/Role Matrix, Application Delivery Diagram, and Application and Usage Location Diagram.

SCENARIO SET #2 ANSWER KEYS

SCENARIO #9 Jetstream Hydrocycles #1

Topic		Preliminary Phase
Subjects/Rationale		The student should know how to conduct the tasks in the Preliminary Phase
Most Correct	A	Meets the requirements set in the TOGAF® book for the Preliminary Phase.
Second Best	B	There is no Risk Impact Assessment and the Business Transition Readiness Assessment is done in Phase A
Third Best	C	Some of the answers are taken from Phase A
Distractor	D	Some of the answers are taken from Phase A and Requirements Management. It also does not address many of the issues.

SCENARIO #10 Jetstream Hydrocycles #2

Topic		Business Transformation Readiness Assessment
Subjects/Rationale		The student should know how to assess readiness factors
Most Correct	D	This answer follows the content in section 30.4 of the TOGAF® book
Second Best	C	The vision must include the baseline as well as the target architectures.
Third Best	B	The readiness assessment takes place in Phase A.
Distractor	A	These are basically all of the steps in Phase A and do not answer the question.

SCENARIO #11 Jetstream Hydrocycles #3

Topic		
Subjects/Rationale		The student should know how to properly conduct the Architecture Development Iteration.
Most Correct	B	These are the steps across all three of the phases for conducting the Architecture Development Iteration.
Second Best	D	This answer leaves out the Gap Analysis and adds documentation found only in the Data Architecture outputs.
Third Best	A	The gap analysis in this answer belongs in each of the phases B-D. Phase E is where the analyses are reviewed and gaps closed.
Distractor	C	This answer has many problems and does not answer the question.

SCENARIO #12 Jetstream Hydrocycles #4

Topic		Phase E: Opportunities and Solutions
Subjects/Rationale		The student should recognize and understand the concept of the elements required to build the draft Implementation and Migration Plan.
Most Correct	D	These are the steps, some with detail, in the TOGAF® book for conducting Phase E
Second Best	C	This is all correct except the Implementation and Migration Plan is not low-level at the end of Phase E.
Third Best	B	There are elements from Phase F in this answer; there is no such thing as a mid-level Implementation and Migration Plan
Distractor	A	This answer does not address the stakeholder concerns and contains elements from both Phase E and Phase F as well as other invalid answers.

SCENARIO #13 Jetstream Hydrocycles #5

Topic		Phase F: Migration and Planning
Subjects/Rationale		The student should know how to conduct the steps necessary to prepare for the architecture transition implementation.
Most Correct	B	These answers are found in the TOGAF® steps for Phase F.
Second Best	A	"Requests for Information and Multiple Organization Enterprises" is not a valid statement. A business transition readiness assessment is not completed in this Phase.
Third Best	C	The Implementation and Migration Plan is only a draft at the beginning of this Phase. It is at version 1.0 at the completion. Other partially correct answers.
Distractor	D	Most of the elements in this answer are wrong.

SCENARIO #14 Jetstream Hydrocycles #6

Topic		Architecture Capability Iteration
Subjects/Rationale		The student should know how to conduct an Architecture Capability iteration in response to changes.
Most Correct	B	This answer provides the most relevant steps to address changes needed to align the implementation according to the needs of the enterprise as opposed to the wants of politically connected stakeholders.
Second Best	C	This answer leaves out a vital step: introducing an Architecture Principle for Fairness, which seeks to avoid undue influence of certain stakeholders. Redefining and reorganizing the EA team and determining business constraints for implementation are not exactly relevant.
Third Best	A	Steps are not in the correct order according to the ADM cycle structure; a principle for Responsibility does not hit the mark for this issue as well as Fairness.
Distractor	D	This answer does not provide a coherent solution to the problem at hand.

SCENARIO #15 Jetstream Hydrocycles #7

Topic		Change Management
Subjects/Rationale		The student should know how to make changes to the architecture to meet new technology developments.
Most Correct	C	This is the most complete and correct answer
Second Best	D	The views detailed in the Application and Data Architecture phases are confused with each other.
Third Best	A	An iteration of phase C is required because every element of the architecture needs to at least be evaluated for the effect of new elements.
Distractor	B	The directive was for the Solutions Architect to conduct an iteration of the Architecture Development Iteration, not to work the Architecture Capability Iteration.

SCENARIO #16 Jetstream Hydrocycles #8

Topic		Architecture Content Framework: Metamodel Extensions
Subjects/Rationale		This scenario addresses the identification of the correct Metamodel Extension to solve a problem. In this case, the Infrastructure Consolidation Extensions.
Most Correct	A	This follows the guidelines set in Part IV, Section 34.4, Content Metamodel Extensions
Second Best	B	Metamodel Extensions are identified in the Architecture Vision Phase
Third Best	C	The extensions listed are in other metamodel extension sections
Distractor	D	This answer does not correctly identify any answers to the concerns

Set 3: Scenarios 17 - 24

SCENARIO #17 Langsam Shipping

BACKGROUND

Langsam Shipping is an international delivery corporation that comprises ships, rail, and lorry freight shipping. Langsam has been an industry leader for three decades and enjoys a healthy financial reputation and is responsible for 18% of all lorry shipping, 13% of freight rail, and 13% of ship transport globally. The enterprise is undergoing a major IT architectural transition to streamline its substantial information systems reach. With data centers located in several countries, they are now moving their IT infrastructure into just three data centers: one in the US, one in UK, and one in China. This will relieve them of $25 million dollars in capital and operational expenses in the next 5 years. They have a very mature Enterprise Architecture team that has successfully transitioned their US data center.

Over the past several months, the executive team has researched the opportunities offered by cloud services, which would drastically reduce CAPEX and OPEX from what was previously initiated. With that kind of promise, they realized that not only was it a better option, but that halting the current transition and re-architecting the entire solution would have an upfront cost which would pay for itself after the first year of the end of all three phases.

The only thing that concerns them is the risk that these changes will be conducted with a minimum of cost and time. They have convened a meeting of the Board of Directors and invited you, the Chief Architect, to review with them what measures you have taken to insure this kind of change would have the positive results that they desire.

QUESTION

Refer to the scenario

Your role is the Chief Architect.

You are about to present to the Board of Directors what your estimation of these changes will do to the transition and how you would ease their concerns. Your presentation consists of the way in which you instituted a healthy governance framework that prepared the transition for this kind of change.

Based on TOGAF® 9, which of the following is the best answer?

ANSWERS

A. Establish global and local governance boards, select design authorities and working parties. Organize the structure of the governance framework for the migration plan: Enterprise Architects will develop; Program Managers will implement; and Service Managers will deploy. Assign members to the cross-functional Architecture Board. Establish a comprehensive set of architecture principles, and adopt an architecture compliance strategy.

B. Identify members to an Architecture Board. Allow for approvals of dispensational change requests. Take on policy management processes. Organize the structure of the governance framework for the migration plan: Enterprise Architects will develop; Program Managers will implement; and Service Managers will deploy and adopt an architecture compliance strategy.

C. Confirm management framework interactions for implementation and migration plan; assign a business value to each work package; estimate resource requirements, project timings, and availability/delivery vehicle; prioritize the migration projects through the conduct of a cost/benefit assessment and risk validation; confirm architecture roadmap and update architecture definition document; complete the implementation and migration plan; and complete the architecture development cycle and document lessons learned.

D. Confirm scope and priorities for deployment with development management; identify resources and skills; guide development of solutions deployment; perform enterprise architecture reviews; implement business and IT operations; perform post-implementation review and close the implementation; publish the signed architecture contract, compliance assessments, changes requests, and architecture-compliant solutions deployed.

SCENARIO #18 NSW Air Frequent Flyer Mile System

BACKGROUND

NSW Air is an international airline with a network of domestic and intercontinental routes mainly in the Asia-Pacific region. In addition, NSW Air operates a catering service and provides travel and holiday tourism services throughout Australia. NSW Air provides electronic reservation systems, ground handling, and engineering and maintenance services. NSW Air flies to 20 domestic destinations and 21 international destinations in 14 countries across Africa, the Americas, Asia, Europe and Oceania excluding the destinations served by its subsidiaries. In the entire NSW Air group it serves 60 domestic and 27 international destinations. Domestically, NSW Air advertises all direct flights between the mainland state capital cities Adelaide, Brisbane, Melbourne, Perth and Sydney, and the national capital Canberra.

NSW Air has a mature enterprise architecture practice and uses TOGAF® 9 for the basis of the NSW Air Architecture Framework (method and deliverables).

NSW Air executives have directed the Information Technology Services team (ITS) to move its massive frequent flyer program onto a cloud-based computing platform in order to keep up with growing demand. An InstiTute Database service incorporating a scalable architecture designed to cope with changes in demand will replace its 22-year-old COBOL based system. The system will be able to provide consistent service to some seven million members, while also dealing with rapidly growing activity. NSW Air also sees the new platform as providing the opportunity to target loyalty promotions and extend its loyalty program by introducing new partners—something that would have been difficult with the older system.

At the most recent meeting of the Corporate Board, the Chairman of the Board expressed a concern about the risk of communications disruptions with their Frequent Flyer Mile partners as the program is under transition. He noted that several code-share partners have held off implementing the same strategy but have so far held back because of this very reason.

QUESTION

Refer to the scenario

Your role is the Chief Architect.

You have been asked to present how you plan to mitigate the risks of these concerns during transition.

Based on TOGAF® 9, which of the following is the best answer?

ANSWERS

A. You will assign each member of the EA a specific risk to control and mitigate. That person will report directly to you with information about the discovery of the risk so you will be able to meet with the Board of Directors to determine a course of action. Based on their decision, you will proceed with the implementation as planned, but only after the risk has been eliminated. In no case will risks be allowed to become residual or their solutions have negative side effects to the plan. At the end of reaching each transition architecture, reassign the risks to different EA team members to ensure a level of cross-functioning knowledge sharing.

B. After establishing the Architecture Definitions for Business, Information Systems, and Technology, the EA team will conduct an assessment for readiness to identify the risks to failure of the implementation. Your team will use ABBs in past projects, which addressed communications between code-share systems, and tailor them for new SBBs in the solution development. You will create a Risk Classification Matrix to classify risks according to the effect they will have, their expected frequency, and the level of risk for each. The solution will have built-in redundancies and fallbacks and the implementation will be closely watched using best practices based review methods.

C. During Governance, as a solid method for insuring that the implementation proceeds without failure, the Architecture Review Board will: review migration planning outputs and produce recommendations on deployment; identify deployment issues and make recommendations; identify building blocks for replacement, update, etc.; perform gap analysis on enterprise architecture and solutions framework; and review ongoing implementation governance and architecture compliance for each building block. The solution will have built-in redundancies and fallbacks and the implementation will be closely watched using best practices based review methods.

D. Present to the board that you expect that risks will be identified as a result of readiness assessments. The EA team will focus on those that most affect continuity of service and inter-airline communications. They will watch for gaps that would preclude reaching interim transition points as well as reaching the final target architecture. You will create a Risk Classification Matrix to classify risks according to the effect they will have, their expected frequency, and the level of risk for each. The solution will have built-in redundancies and fallbacks and the implementation will be closely watched using best practices based review methods.

SCENARIO #19 Parson F&HG, Inc. Scenario #1

BACKGROUND

Parson F&HG, together with its subsidiaries, provides consumer packaged goods and improves the lives of consumers worldwide. The company operates through six segments: Beauty, Grooming, Health Care, Pet Care, Fabric Care and Home Care, and Baby Care and Family Care. Over the past three months, the corporation set forth a plan to homogenize several internal processes among the myriad subsidiaries to create efficiencies using common tools, applications, and procedures and realize about $15 million in savings over 4 years. Parson engaged a consulting firm, JONF, to help analyze the enterprise architecture, make recommendations for architectural changes, and conduct the creation of a robust enterprise architecture based on TOGAF® 9.1.

JONF's first recommendation was to establish an effective communications architecture. Their reasoning was that by creating this architecture first, they would have better results gathering information among the many divisions for later architecture development.

JONF has contracted you and your team of experienced Enterprise Architects to take on this initial program with the premise that if you successfully completed this first project, they would select your firm for the rest of the architecture transformation expected to last 4 years.

QUESTION

Refer to the scenario

Your role is the Chief Architect.

You have been asked to execute the plan recommended by JONF. Based on TOGAF® 9, which of the following is the best way to begin this project?

ANSWERS

A. Create a round table of co-sponsors to act as the definitive authority for the program over watch. Make sure that they are cross representative of a selection of various sizes and locations of the subsidiaries to preclude preferential consideration. This will also assure continuity over the 4 years. Assign the co-sponsors the responsibility of producing documentation of the current cultural environments, styles of communication, and lists of the most to least effective division communications programs. Then the co-sponsors will create an Architecture Vision that will: set the budget, the timeline, the selection of personnel from each division, and their roles and responsibilities. In parallel, have your team establish the Architecture Principles, which will be part of the Architecture Vision.

B. Encourage the CEO to be the program sponsor to be intimately involved from the beginning of the program to assure continuity throughout the 4-year program regardless of the EA firm that will be selected to complete it. Given the potentially disparate communications processes among the subsidiaries, define the sole language to be used to be English. This will mitigate confusion when addressing specific elements of the architecture as it rolls out globally. Establish a set of documented Architecture Principles. Finally, produce the Statement of Architecture Work.

C. Identify yourself as the program sponsor with the provision that you will fully document the first project (to establish the Communications Architecture) and hand the work to the following Chief Architect should you not be selected to continue. Get a full understanding of the impact on core, soft, extended entities, and other communities that will be impacted by the program. Gain an understanding of the cultural differences between divisions. Establish a set of documented Architecture Principles. Finally, produce the Request for Architecture Work and finalize the Architecture Vision.

D. Because of the scope of the project (covering a multitude of semi-independent global enterprises), you ask for and receive a program sponsor to be intimately involved from the beginning of the program to assure continuity throughout the 4-year program regardless of the EA firm that will be selected to complete it. Obtain a commitment to a specific budget. Get a full understanding of the impact on core, soft, extended entities, and other communities that will be impacted by the program. Gain an understanding of the cultural differences between divisions. Establish a set of documented Architecture Principles. Finally, produce the Request for Architecture Work.

SCENARIO #20 Parson F&HG, Inc. Scenario #2

BACKGROUND

Parson F&HG, together with its subsidiaries, provides consumer packaged goods and improves the lives of consumers worldwide. The company operates through six segments: Beauty, Grooming, Health Care, Pet Care, Fabric Care and Home Care, and Baby Care and Family Care. Early last year, the corporation set forth a plan to homogenize several internal processes among the myriad subsidiaries to create efficiencies using common tools, applications, and procedures and realize about $15 million in savings over 4 years. Parson engaged a consulting firm, JONF, to help analyze the enterprise architecture, make recommendations for architectural changes, and conduct the creation of a robust enterprise architecture based on TOGAF® 9.1.

JONF's first recommendation was to establish an effective communications architecture, which was successfully completed. The next program would be to implement two core processes for the enterprises: unified inventory tracking and reporting. The problems inherent in producing these processes are the obvious differences between subsidiary business models and regional/cultural environments. Over the years, individual subsidiaries have taken on this task with sometimes disastrous, costly results. Some of that was due to personnel not experienced in architecture development; some was due to lack of governance during implementation. In fact, there was no Architecture Board to regulate governance, and the change management structure was ineffective.

JONF contracted you and your team of experienced Enterprise Architects to design and implement this program. Your firm was responsible for the communications architecture development, so you can easily gain access to the various divisions for detailed information on organizational, regional and cultural differences. This should help to mitigate the problems in past attempts. Your firm has now completed the Architectural Development and Transition Planning iterations.

QUESTION

Refer to the scenario.

Your role is the Chief Architect.

Based on TOGAF® 9, which of the following is the best way to continue the implementation?

ANSWERS

A. Confirm management framework interactions for Implementation and Migration. Assign a business value to each work package. Estimate resource requirements. Prioritize the migration projects by conducting a cost/benefit analysis and risk assessment. Confirm the Architecture Roadmap and update the Architecture Definition Document. Complete the Implementation Plan and finalize the construction of a durable change management program. Complete the Architecture Development cycle and document lessons learned.

B. Establish an implementation program to deliver the transition as agreed upon in Phase F. Identify individuals to be educated with the appropriate skills and deployed as needed. Document the Architecture Contract, obtaining signatures from all developing organizations and sponsoring organization. Update the Enterprise Continuum directory and repository for solutions. Publish architecture compliance recommendations and dispensations and recommendations on performance metrics. Finalize the Architecture Vision after implementation.

C. Establish an implementation program to deliver the transition as agreed upon in Phase F. Define the operations framework to ensure long life of deployed solution. Continually monitor the performance of the implementation. Perform enterprise architecture compliance reviews. Monitor changes in technology and business that may impact the baseline architecture. Establish a well-defined change management process and an authoritative change management office. Assess change requests and reporting to ensure that the expected SLAs are met. Ensure change management requests adhere to the enterprise architecture governance and framework.

D. Establish business projects to exploit the enterprise architecture for value realization. Monitor enterprise Architecture Capability maturity. Establish a change review board with hardened rules for resistance to changes that will have too many residual risks. Continually monitor for interoperation communications between subdivisions between subsidiaries. Analyze performance and undertake a gap analysis of performance against the established criteria. Produce the appropriate documentation such as a new Request for Architecture Work, a Statement of Architecture Work, the Architecture Contract and Compliance Assessments

SCENARIO #21 Devon Martin Frozen Foods

BACKGROUND

Devon Martin Frozen Foods (DMFF) is brand of frozen prepared foods available in the United States and Canada. DMFF is known for such popular fare as meatloaf, Salisbury steak, lasagna, macaroni and cheese, and ravioli. It also produces a line of reduced-fat products under the banner "DM Getting Lean!" DMFF also launched the Family Dinner campaign around 2010. This campaign focused on bringing families together around the dinner table in order to share a meal. DMFF used a variety of marketing techniques in order to help gain awareness for this new campaign. The use of the Internet and print ads was incorporated in order to hit a wide audience. An online survey, webisodes, blogging round table, Facebook, and Twitter were all used online as a way to spread the word. This marketing technique used social media websites as a way to better market their new campaign.

DFMM Marketing has presented a new, radical direction for the food producing firm: Take-out and Deliver storefronts along the lines of some key pizza restaurants. The marketing team did a focus group study in Des Moines, IA, which resulted in an optimistic report encouraging them to unfold the program to the executive leadership and board of directors. Eventually, these stakeholders agreed to a pilot store in Des Moines to test market acceptability. An Enterprise Architecture Contractor was engaged to take on the implementation of the pilot project. The ADM Cycle was initiated and has gone through two iterations of the Architecture Development phases, and the initial iteration of the Transition Planning phases.

While the Architecture Board was reviewing the end results of Phase F, a food industry magazine revealed that a competitor had successfully implemented a similar market strategy in Oregon and Washington State. They had already built 20 stores and the results were exceeding expectations. This news caused great concern and the Board of Directors recommended that the pilot project be scrapped and for the company to move forward with the full implementation with 5 stores in the Des Moines MSA. The executive team and major stakeholders agreed to proceed but with trepidation. They were concerned that the development phases would need to be reiterated with a new Statement of Architecture to insure that the dynamics implied by the change would be fully vetted.

QUESTION

Refer to the scenario.

Your role is the Chief Architect.

You now have to halt the Transition Planning iteration and proceed with the new direction.

Based on TOGAF® 9, which of the following is the best answer?

ANSWERS

A. Add the new requirements and modify the existing requirements as necessary. The architects responsible for current phase, with oversight from the relevant stakeholders, will re-assess priorities based on the re-established requirements. Assess the impact of the changes to the requirements on previous phases. Issue a Requirements Impact Statement version n+1. Implement the requirements changes arising from Phase H. Update the Requirements Repository with the information from the changes, including the stakeholder views affected. Conduct a Gap Analysis for the current Phase and the side effects on other phases. If there are significant changes, begin an iteration of the Architecture Capability Iteration and restart the ADM cycle.

B. Restart the ADM cycle beginning with the Preliminary Phase. Add the new requirements and modify the existing requirements as necessary. The architects responsible for current phase, with oversight from the relevant stakeholders, will re-assess priorities based on the re-established requirements. Assess the impact of the changes to the requirements on previous phases. Issue a Requirements Impact Statement version n+1. Implement the requirements changes arising from Phase H. Update the Requirements Repository with the information from the changes, including the stakeholder views affected. Conduct a Gap Analysis for the current Phase and the side effects on other phases.

C. Restart the ADM cycle beginning with the Preliminary Phase. Add the new requirements and modify the existing requirements as necessary. The architects responsible for current phase, with oversight from the relevant stakeholders, will re-assess priorities based on the re-established requirements. Scope the enterprise organizations impacted. Confirm governance and support frameworks. Define and establish enterprise architecture team and organization. Identify Stakeholders, Concerns, and Business Requirements. Identify the business goals and strategic drivers of the organization. Assess the work products that are required against the set of business performance requirements.

D. Add the new requirements and modify the existing requirements as necessary. The architects responsible for current phase, with oversight from the relevant stakeholders, will re-assess priorities based on the re-established requirements. Assess the impact of the changes to the requirements on previous phases. Prepare a Statement of Architecture Work and Architecture Development Structure document. After conducting an iteration of the Architecture Capability

Iteration, proceed to conducting Phases B-D to re-state and re-establish the four domain requirements. Follow this with a completed Architecture Definition Document and Architecture Roadmap before beginning the new Transition Planning Iteration.

SCENARIO #22 DayForm Mutual Insurance

BACKGROUND

DayForm Mutual Insurance Company is an American mutual insurance company, which sells automobile, homeowners, marine and personal umbrella liability insurance, founded in 1937. It employs 1,224 people in 20 offices across the United States, and is headquartered in Lincoln, Nebraska. DayForm is one of the few remaining large-scale mutual insurance firms that consistently highly ranked in JD Power and other consumer satisfaction rankings. After attending a global conference on Cloud Computing, the CEO and CIO began a review of the cost-benefits of migrating their technology platform to this new service-oriented architecture. The CEO's vision is to move to two sets of metrics: customer satisfaction and key business performance indicators. He tasked the CIO with creating a plan to realize the vision.

DayForm does not have an Enterprise Architecture Framework, but the CIO is familiar with its advantages and impressed with the results he has seen in a competitor's adaptation of TOGAF® 9.1 into their environment. He contracted with a well-known EA consulting firm to begin the ADM Cycle. He realizes there will be shareholder resistance to this change and that there is a silo mentality among the disparate divisions. The CFO is very concerned about the short-term financial impact and needs assurance that the transition can be spread out over a long enough period to have as little impact to quarterly reports.

QUESTION

Refer to the scenario.

Your role is the Chief Architect.

You have been asked to convince the major stakeholders that the activities of the EA team will have a low impact to the corporation's day-to-day operations and will satisfy the CFO's concerns. You have completed the Request for Architecture Work and are now working on the Architecture Vision, and to present the Statement of Architecture Work for approval.

Based on TOGAF® 9.1, which of the following is the best approach?

ANSWERS

A. Document clearly the concerns, visions, and constraints of each stakeholder in the enterprise; conduct a Business Transformation Readiness Assessment; invite stakeholders into the business scenario exercises; create high level Baseline and Target Architectures; get buy-in from the stakeholders on the business value of the transition; identify risks; create the draft Statement of Architecture Work. When presenting the SAW, emphasize a measured approach to the implementation.

B. Define the scope of the enterprise, the architecture principles, and the frameworks to be used; tailor TOGAF® to the current architecture framework; create the Architecture Vision; train the EA team member liaisons from the company; run business scenarios with involvement from the stakeholder teams; create high level Baseline and Target Architectures; document the business value of the new architecture; create the draft Statement of Work.

C. Establish the Business Phases to be implemented in reference to their milestones; create business architecture principles, write the Architecture Project Vision; delegate several division liaisons to act as points of contact during the Architecture Development Cycle, the Transition Cycle, and to sit on the Architecture Review board during the Implementation Governance Cycle. Extract ABBs from the Enterprise Continuum to create SBBs in the final Statement of Architecture Work. When presenting the SAW, emphasize a measured approach to the implementation.

D. Define the scope of the enterprise along divisional lines; define the architectural principles based on existing business principles; describe the value of the solution using a cost-benefit analysis; create detailed Baseline and Target Architectures; create a new Request for Architecture Work document, the Architecture Vision, and a draft Statement of Architecture Work. When presenting the SAW, emphasize a measured approach to the implementation.

SCENARIO #23 Better Bitters (BBS GmbH)

BACKGROUND

Better Bitters (BBS GmbH) is a global conglomeration of manufacturers of beers, lagers, and ales. They own six brewery companies in seventeen markets in the US, Canada, EU, and Asia-Pacific. Over the past 3 years, the company has completed a mostly successful completion of establishing an enterprise architecture practice based on TOGAF®. However, the program was only able to obtain 90% of the goals set due to intractable technology infrastructure issues and data capture inconsistencies.

For instance, Breweries in Romania and Slovakia had such an outdated technology infrastructure that modernizing them had become problematic; some locations could not be upgraded during this program. The Hungarian brewery's data had never been translated into one of the major languages.

These obstacles had caused the Request for Architecture Work to be restated three times and the program budget was exceeded by 300%. As a result, major stakeholders, especially those in Eastern Europe, expressed dissatisfaction with the program; they felt they were "out of the loop" by not being included on the Architecture Board, which was a major reason for cost overruns.

Recently, BBS acquired two manufacturers of ales in Australia, and, following the guidance of the Architecture Board, began an iteration of the ADM cycle. The EA teams had completed the Architecture Development Iteration and were preparing the Transition Planning Iteration when BBS announced the acquisition of one more brewery, this time in Ireland.

The BBS Architecture Board, after intense internal negotiations, has decided to put implementation on hold to wait for the inclusion of the new acquisition into the architecture migration at hand. The stakeholders, while generally supportive of the EA effort, are highly sensitive to the planning of the revised program based on the past execution. Their three major mandates are:

- F. Careful attention to keeping within or below budget
- G. Flawless evaluation of existing technology and data baseline architectures
- H. Increased stakeholder involvement

QUESTION

Refer to the scenario.

The Chief Architect has assembled the enterprise architecture team—now a mature, experienced organization—and briefed them on the situation. He has instructed them to make every effort to prevent the past recycles and cost overruns. He also emphasized the necessity of complete transparency to the stakeholders. The new Request for Architecture Work and Architecture Vision deliverables have been completed and the Architecture Development Iterations are about to begin. The stakeholders in Ireland have been fully incorporated into the Architecture Review process.

You have been designated as the Lead Architect for the program. As you consider the plan for the execution of the Architecture Development Iteration, based on TOGAF® 9, which answer below highlights the aspects of the plan that best addresses the stakeholder concerns?

ANSWERS

A. The Lead Architect will direct his team to quickly identify gaps between the existing data and technology environments of the new acquisition. Solutions Building Blocks can then be applied directly to the elements of the new site without cumbersome and redundant exercises. This will greatly reduce time in production. To alleviate the concerns of the stakeholders, the EA team will invite a representative to help with the details of the program; this person will report back on a daily basis to the rest of the stakeholders. Before beginning the Migration Planning Phase, the Lead Architect will present to the Architecture Review Board the substance of the Baseline architecture findings, the finalized Target architecture, and the Transition Architecture giving them an opportunity to flag concerns before proceeding with Implementation Planning

B. The Lead Architect will approach and engage the stakeholders to gather their concerns in detail, document their concerns, and delineate how the Transition Architecture will address the concerns. In the Architecture Definition iterations, great care must be taken to determine the exact state of technology and data environment before closing the gaps between the baseline and target architectures. Gaps should be carefully scrutinized and the end of each phase should end with the acceptance of the stakeholders to move to the next step. After creating the Transition Plan in Phase E, the EA team will complete the Migration and Planning phase after which they will get final approval from the CEO to proceed with the Architecture Governance Iteration.

C. The EA team should first complete the implementation of the two companies in progress with a parallel development of the Transition Architecture of the new one. The parallel projects will speed time to production, not confusing the disparate elements between the two thereby reducing the risk of continued reiteration. In the development of the new program, the team will be able to concentrate on a simplified effort in developing the separate Transition Architecture and would have the benefit of lessons learned from the previous migration. . Before beginning the Migration Planning Phase, the Lead Architect will present to the Architecture Review Board the substance of the Baseline architecture findings, the finalized Target architecture, and the Transition Architecture giving them an opportunity to flag concerns before proceeding with Implementation Planning

D. In the first iteration of Architecture Definition, the EA team must ensure that in Phase C, they must closely review the data stores for compatibility to the corporate data and application architectures. In Phase D, the Technology Architecture must diligently evaluate the baseline technologies in place, ascertaining any gaps in the existing environment. In the second iteration of Architecture Definition, the EA team will identify gaps between the Baseline and Target architectures. In Phase E, they will close the gaps between Baseline and Target. The creation of the Transition Architecture will then be finalized. Before beginning the Migration Planning Phase, the Lead Architect will present to the Architecture Review Board the substance of the Baseline architecture findings, the finalized Target architecture, and the Transition Architecture giving them an opportunity to flag concerns before proceeding with Implementation Planning.

SCENARIO #24 Adaptation Technologies iNitiatives

BACKGROUND

Adaptation Technologies iNitiatives (ATi) is a software engineering firm that specializes modifying COTS applications to adapt them to customer-specific requirements. Established in 1989, it has enjoyed a most profitable history. The company prides itself in being at the cutting-edge of emerging technology tools, which has helped make it one of the most sought-after companies in its field. With the advent of cloud computing, the executives and board members conferred and unanimously agreed that ATi should immediately begin transitioning their current PC-based computing infrastructure to a hosted one with the assurance that the move would dramatically decrease costs in Capital and Operational expenses. Some of that savings would be used to invest in more software engineers that are needed to expand the business.

They have contracted with HC Enterprise Architects, Inc. (HCEA) to run the transition program and have begun the preparation of the solution. While examining the baseline architecture, the EA team established that the current business services are not well matched to the target technologies. Management operations between PC premise based systems and hosted based systems are divergent. Likewise, governance models will have to be changed in the new architecture. So there are concerns that the transitions of these two elements of the solution will be risky.

QUESTION

Refer to the scenario

Your role is the Chief Architect of HCEA.

You are presently working to address the concerns of the stakeholders.

Based on TOGAF® 9, which of the following is the best answer?

ANSWERS

A. Execute due diligence examining the governance frameworks to fully understand the limitations uncovered as they relate to the projected plan; tailor the governance metamodel with governance extensions since regulatory issues will greatly impact the new governance models; build services extensions because services will be vastly enhanced over the baseline architecture; tailor process modeling extensions to address the importance of tracking specific incidents and events.

B. Execute due diligence examining the governance frameworks to fully understand the limitations uncovered as they relate to the projected plan; tailor the governance metamodel with governance extensions since changes will result in a significant impact to existing operational governance models; build services extensions because the present service definitions are preset and do not align well to the needs of the new architecture.

C. Establish with the stakeholders the consensus to institute guidelines and principles for governance of the program as well as creating a special service oversight team to track service related residual risks. Software engineering practices are a vital part of service tracking so at least one person should be identified to sponsor this part of the solution. Likewise, a representative from the executive team should be included to act as a gate for changes in the governance model.

D. Execute due diligence examining the governance frameworks to fully understand the limitations uncovered as they relate to the projected plan; tailor metamodel extensions addressing compliance reports, service reports, surface gain reports and the software changes needed; establish a repository separate from the Architecture Repository in the Enterprise Continuum to gather software engineering artifacts affecting services.

SCENARIO SET #3 ANSWER KEYS

SCENARIO #17 Langsam Shipping

Topic	Architecture Governance	
Subjects/Rationale	The student must be able to correctly identify how to setup a proper governance framework.	
Most Correct	A	These answers are compliant with section 50 of TOGAF®
Second Best	B	Some of these answers are correct; some are not.
Third Best	C	While these are steps in Phase H, they do not adequately provide the details needed.
Distractor	D	These are steps from Phase G

SCENARIO #18 NSW Air Frequent Flyer Mile System

Topic	Risk Assessment	
Subjects/Rationale	The student must be able to correctly identify how to plan mitigation of risks	
Most Correct	D	The elements of this answer come directly from Risk Management
Second Best	B	Risk Management must be addressed before the beginning of Architecture Development
Third Best	C	All of the elements of this answer occur in the Implementation Governance phase, but only slightly address risk implementation
Distractor	A	This answer does not follow TOGAF® in any way.

SCENARIO #19 Parson F&HG, Inc. Scenario #1

Topic		Preliminary Phase
Subjects/Rationale		The student must be able to understand the steps involved in preparing for an iteration of the ADM
Most Correct	D	This answer follows the approach and steps for conducting the Preliminary Phase
Second Best	C	While much of this answer is correct, the Chief Architect, no matter how promising in the commitment to share documentation, should not be the sponsor. The sponsor must be a duly appointed executive with stake in the program's success.
Third Best	B	Some correct answers, but the CEO is not the best choice for sponsorship since the duties of that role are too involved in higher-level strategic decision-making. A CIO would be a better choice. Defining English as the sole language may have merits, but it will likely create resentment in the global branches that you need for this program to succeed.
Distractor	A	There should not be a round table of co-sponsors; this is directly in contradiction of TOGAF®. They also are not to be responsible for gathering information that is the job of the EAs.

SCENARIO #20 Parson F&HG, Inc. Scenario #2

Topic		ADM Phases: Governance
Subjects/Rationale		The student should be able to identify the correct TOGAF® processes and tools for creating effective governance during the implementation of an architecture.
Most Correct	C	This answer provides the correct procedures in Phases G and H, and addresses the stakeholder concerns with an emphasis on Change Management
Second Best	B	This answer only provides the processes in Phase G. Phase H is an integral part of governance because it addresses stakeholder concerns about change management.
Third Best	D	This answer only provides processes in Phase H, is disjointed in its approach, and does not address stakeholder concerns.
Distractor	A	This answer is from Phase F, not a part of governance.

SCENARIO #22 Devon Martin Frozen Foods

Topic		Requirements Management
Subjects/Rationale		The student must be able to recognize the role Requirements Management plays in the ADM
Most Correct	A	This answer follows the steps stated in Requirements Management
Second Best	B	This answer begins without Requirements Management steps and leaves out what the next step would be.
Third Best	C	This answer begins without Requirements Management steps and uses steps from the Preliminary Phase and Phase A.
Distractor	D	This is an unfocused answer.

SCENARIO #22 DayForm Mutual Insurance

Topic		ADM: Phase A Architecture Vision
Subjects/Rationale		The student must be able to identify the appropriate steps in Phase A to address stakeholder concerns and build a solid foundation for the rest of the ADM Cycle.
Most Correct	A	These elements address the overall implementation plans and ensures stakeholder satisfaction
Second Best	B	Half of these elements are from the Preliminary Phase, which has already been completed (Request for Architecture Work).
Third Best	D	An unclear method, not based on TOGAF®
Distractor	C	An undirected and ultimately unfit answer.

SCENARIO #23 Better Bitters (BBS GmbH)

Topic		Architecture Definition; Architecture Repository
Subjects/Rationale		The scenario emphasizes stakeholder management, use of ABBs, and data compatibility. It has a wide range of areas for consideration.
Most Correct	D	This answer includes actions necessary to alleviate the concerns in the right sequence.
Second Best	B	Stakeholder selection would already have been completed by the time Architecture Definition began, and the Lead Architect would not be able to present the Transition Architecture at this time. Approval to being migration is normally a function of the Architecture Review Board, not a C-level executive.
Third Best	A	Not all of the concerns are addressed. The Lead Architect's priority seems to be on speed of execution rather than on excellence of execution.
Distractor	C	The EA team does not have the authority to override the Architecture Review Board.

SCENARIO #24 Adaptation Technologies iNitiatives

Topic		Architecture Content Framework: Metamodel Extensions
Subjects/Rationale		The student should be able to identify the proper way to apply extensions to the metamodel appropriately
Most Correct	B	The Governance and Services extensions address the concerns of the stakeholders and are correctly applied.
Second Best	A	The Governance and Services extensions are correctly identified, but not for the reasons stated; process modeling extensions to not apply to stakeholder concerns.
Third Best	D	The reference to tailoring metamodel extensions is too vague; a separate repository is not appropriate and does not comply with TOGAF®.
Distractor	C	Interesting read but does not address any of the issues presented.

Set 4: Scenarios 25-32

SCENARIO #25 Amsterdam Chemical

BACKGROUND

Amsterdam Chemical is a struggling industrial chemical manufacturer and distributor in specialty chemicals delivering products and solutions to sectors such as electronics, water, and energy. At the last shareholder meeting, it was made clear to the board of directors that their confidence was waning and that if the company did not return a profit within the next 12 months, they would evaluate a sale of the firm. Up until this time, the CEO, CFO, and CTO had been asking the board for their support to invest in an overhaul of their enterprise architecture. Their contention was that doing so would eliminate waste and bring higher productivity. They believed that they could establish a culture of transparency by elimination of duplicated and unnecessary processes, and flattening out legacy silo organizations. They asserted that this would remove some of the expenses of running the organization. In the long run it was their collective opinion that as the architecture changed profitability would rise.

With the shareholders providing the pressure for change, the Board acquiesced to their plan. The executives began meetings with all of the Vice Presidents and Directors to communicate their vision. They contracted a reputable team of enterprise architects to educate the stakeholders on what Enterprise Architecture is and what demands it will make on everyone in the company. While many of the stakeholders were reticent to this plan, the general atmosphere was one of cooperation. There were two directors with stringent demands for transparency during the execution of the ADM.

Directors for the Software Development and the Technology Organizations expressed a desire to be provided all documentation concerning details directly related to functional design elements during the Architecture Capability and Architecture Development Iterations.

QUESTION

Refer to the scenario.

You are the Lead Architect and liaison to the stakeholders.

Based on TOGAF® 9, which of the following provides the best answer to satisfying the requirements of the Directors?

ANSWERS

A. During Phase A, meet with the directors to review the Organizational Model for Enterprise Architecture and Request for Assessment Work; in Phase B, examine the Architecture Protocols; Business Vision; Business Principles, Goals, and Drivers; finalized Tailored Architecture Framework; and the Statement of Architecture Work. In Phases C-D, specify the Communications Plan, Compliance Assessment, and finalized Architecture Roadmap. In Phases E and F complete the evaluation by covering the finalized Governance Implementation Plan and

Solution Building Blocks (SBBs) from Phases B-D, and share the Initial Architecture Repository and completed Requirements Management Plan.

B. During the Preliminary Phase, present to the directors the Tailored Architecture Framework and Request for Architecture Work; in Phase A, examine: the Capability Assessment; the Architecture Vision; the Business Principles, Goals, and Drivers; the finalized Tailored Architecture Framework; the Statement of Architecture Work; and the Value Chain Diagram. Between the iterations of Phases B-D, review the changes to the Architecture Definition Document, Architecture Requirements Specification, and Statement of Architecture Work. During the Transition Planning Iteration review the finalized Architecture Definition Document and Architecture Requirements Specification from Phases B-D, and share the completed Communications Plan.

C. During the Preliminary Phase, present to the directors the Organizational Model for Enterprise Architecture and Request for Architecture Work; in Phase A, examine: the Initial Architecture Repository; the Architecture Vision; the Business Principles, Goals, and Drivers; the finalized Tailored Architecture Framework; and the Statement of Architecture Work. Throughout the iterations of Phases B-D, review the changes to the Architecture Definition Document, Architecture Governance Framework, Statement of Architecture Work, and Principles Catalog. During the Transition Planning Iteration review the finalized Architecture Definition Document and Architecture Requirements Specification from Phases B-D, and share the completed Governance and support strategy.

D. During the Preliminary Phase, present to the directors the Tailored Architecture Framework and Request for Architecture Work; in Phase A, examine: the Architecture Vision; the Business Principles, Goals, and Drivers; the finalized Tailored Architecture Framework; and the Statement of Architecture Work. In the iterations of Phases B-D, review the changes to the Architecture Definition Document, Architecture Requirements Specification, and Statement of Architecture Work. During the Transition Planning Iteration review the finalized Architecture Definition Document and Architecture Requirements Specification from Phases B-D, and share the completed Implementation and Migration Plan.

SCENARIO #26 Forth-Write Construction

BACKGROUND

Forth-Write Construction is a major highway construction contractor involved in hundreds of projects from county road repairs to Interstate construction. Until recently, F-WC has operated the company as a collection of several smaller business units each specializing in separate classes of construction. They have known for some time that this model is prone to duplication of efforts, which drains the company's profits. Furthermore, lines of communication are in a constant flux and prone to political mismanagement. But there is also an agreement in the executive staff that trying to merge all of the business units into a single, centrally managed enterprise would stifle productivity. Therefore, the CEO has directed that F-WC restructure its architecture to reflect the diversity of the enterprise balanced with a unity of purpose.

The CEO hired a seasoned Enterprise Architect as CIO who has scoped each of the business units, consulted with their Vice Presidents, and their governance frameworks. The CIO brought with him a mature EA team. They met with the stakeholders and worked out a set of principles that establish the vision of unity and diversity. They have reviewed TOGAF® and tailored it to meet the needs of the enterprise.

The CEO and stakeholders believe that each of the business units have been successfully run, each making profits and maintaining realization of their sales funnels. They see them as very capably run and executed and do not want that inertia slowed during the transition. As they see it, in fact, capabilities should increase as the company rationalizes duplication and that improved communication will establish intra-unit cooperation not seen up to this point.

QUESTION

Refer to the scenario

Your role is the Chief Architect. You will need to ensure that the enterprise maintains its capabilities from the baseline through transition and into the target architectures.

Based on TOGAF® 9, which of the following is the best way to accomplish that?

ANSWERS

A. Conduct a Business Transformation Readiness Assessment to compare against business capability goals and objectives. In the Requirements Management Phase, use the assessment as a basis for corporate capability planning portfolios. The EA team will extract them from the Architecture Repository during the Gap Analyses steps in Phases B-D. Manage and create the outcome-oriented capabilities required to meet the project requirements. These will be used in the Architecture Capability Iteration to create work packages for corporate projects across portfolios. The transitions should consist of capability increments established in Phases E-H to create corporate project work packages across portfolios.

B. Conduct a Business Transformation Readiness Assessment to compare against business transformation goals and objectives. In the Preliminary Phase, use this as a basis for corporate capability planning portfolios to use during the Gap Analyses steps in Phases B-D. Create and manage the outcome-oriented capabilities to meet the project requirements in the Architecture Development Iteration. These capabilities will be the basis for creating work packages for corporate projects across portfolios. The transitions should consist of capability increments established in Phases E and F to create corporate project work packages across portfolios.

C. Develop a corporate strategic plan with business transformation goals and objectives. In the Architecture Vision Phase, use this as a basis for corporate project portfolios and to use during the Architecture Development Iteration. Create and manage the outcome-oriented capabilities to meet the project requirements in the Architecture Development Iteration. These capabilities will be the basis for creating work packages for corporate projects across portfolios. The transitions should consist of capability increments established in Phases E and F to create corporate project work packages across portfolios.

D. Develop a corporate strategic plan with business transformation goals and objectives. In the Preliminary Phase, use this as a basis for corporate project portfolios and to use during the Architecture Vision Phase. Manage and create the outcome-oriented capabilities required to meet the project requirements to be used in the Transition Planning Iteration to create work packages for corporate projects across portfolios. The transitions should consist of capability increments established in Phases E and F to create corporate project work packages across portfolios.

SCENARIO #27 GB Hospitals

BACKGROUND

GB Hospitals is a national group of healthcare providers with locations in 34 states. The enterprise structure is a coagulation of several small healthcare providers that have been undergoing a merger over the past 3 years. Throughout the merger, the each hospital used its own technology infrastructures to handle day-to-day operations. Some inter-hospital communications were setup as a stopgap for information exchange until a holistic solution was implemented. As time passed, lines of communication became exponentially more complex as the temporary solution had to accommodate the increasing number of hospitals in the network.

The situation became critical with a sudden breakdown in communications between 5 hospitals resulting in a critical lack of services to in-patients. Luckily, because of the experience and maturity of hospital staff, there were no major impacts to patient care.

The Board of Directors of GBH called an emergency meeting of the executives to address the situation. There were many issues to resolve including when, who, how, and how much. After three days of deliberation, they agreed unanimously that they would have to incur some debt to engage an Enterprise Architecture consultancy to start work on a strategic solution before further merger activity. The EA consultancy completed the Preliminary Phase and made their pre-ADM cycle meeting with the executives and stakeholders.

The result of the final Request for Architecture Work indicates that there is a great concern that the Target Architecture reconciles the fractured state of communications between people and systems.

QUESTION

Refer to the scenario

You are the Lead Architect. The Chief Architect has briefed you on the concerns of the stakeholders and wants feedback on how you will approach them.

Based on TOGAF® 9, which of the following is the best answer?

ANSWERS

A. Use business scenarios using a Business Transformation Readiness Assessment. Further define them in business terms. Determine the content of the information exchanges. Create an Architecture Definition Increments Table, and a Transition Architecture State Evolution Table. The appropriate technical mechanisms will enable the flow of information from these resources. Refine the Communications Plan in terms of degrees, types, and strategic targets and then update the gap analysis. Determine information exchange requirements using a Business Operation Interoperability Matrix and reconcile the information exchange requirements with potential solutions. Select the solutions that will facilitate the exchanges and build them into the Statement of Architecture Work.

B. Use business scenarios to determine information and service exchange considerations. Further define them in business terms. Determine the content of the information exchanges, how applications are to be shared, and the appropriate technical mechanisms that will enable the flow of information. Refine the information exchange plan in terms of degrees, types, and strategic targets and then update the gap analysis. Use an Implementation Factor Assessment and Deduction Matrix to reconcile the information exchange requirements with potential solutions. Select the solutions that will facilitate the exchanges and build them into the interoperability plan for implementation.

C. Use business scenarios to determine information and service exchange considerations. Further define them in business terms. Determine the content of the information exchanges, how applications are to be shared, and the appropriate technical mechanisms that will enable the flow of information. Refine the information exchange plan in terms of degrees, types, and strategic targets and then update the gap analysis. Use a Business Operation Interoperability Matrix to reconcile the information exchange requirements with potential solutions. Select the solutions that will facilitate the exchanges and build them into the interoperability plan for implementation.

D. Use business scenarios using a Business Transformation Readiness Assessment. Further define them in business terms. Determine the content of the information exchanges, how applications are to be shared, and the appropriate technical mechanisms that will enable the flow of information. Refine the information exchange plan in terms of degrees, types, and strategic targets and then conduct a Gap Analysis. Determine application exchange requirements using a Business Operation Interoperability Matrix. Select the solutions that will facilitate the exchanges and build them into the interoperability plan for implementation. Complete the task with a Transition Architecture State Evolution Table.

SCENARIO #28 Lone Star Beans, Inc.

BACKGROUND

Lone Star Beans is one of the oldest manufacturers of beans in Texas and in many of the surrounding states. It was first established during the end of the westward migrations in the United States. The company is now one of the largest providers of beans in North America, second only to Nuevo Sierra Habichuelas in Mexico. While the product is simple, the manufacturing is complex because of the various species of beans, the large number of recipes, and the range of end products. They also have a mature logistics team that is responsible for distribution in North America as well as an ongoing mission to provide their product to needy populations in the Caribbean such as Haiti and the Dominican Republic.

Lone Star Beans has hired a new CEO who has selected a team of executives to bring the company's technology infrastructure into the 21st century. This goal will modernize production, operations, and logistics into a highly integrated collection of systems working together to establish a Boundaryless Information Flow. To this end, the Executive staff and Board of Directors have engaged the services of a mature Enterprise Architecture company who will lead this endeavor.

The Chief Architect and lead architects have led the executives and stakeholders through the Preliminary Phase of the ADM. Their conversations have revealed that the major concerns of the company's leadership are the transparency of the operation to themselves as well as among the three organizations impacted. They also need to be satisfied that the scope of the solution is strictly maintained to prevent cost overruns.

QUESTION

Refer to the scenario

You are the Chief Architect. During the beginning phases of the ADM you will need to give the stakeholders confidence that their concerns are met.

Based on TOGAF® 9, which of the following is the best way to do that?

ANSWERS

A. In Phase A, create the following artifacts: a Value Chain Diagram to give stakeholders an understanding of the overarching context of the architecture, and a Solution Concept Diagram to establish how the solution meets the objectives. In Phase B, create these artifacts: an Organization/Actor Catalog listing the people that interact with IT, a Driver/Goal/Objective Catalog showing the flexibility of the solution across lines of business, a Role Catalog to identify who is authorized to work in different zones, an Actor/Role Matrix to support the Organization/Actor catalog.

B. In Phase A, create the following artifacts: a Value Chain Diagram to give stakeholders an understanding of the overarching context of the architecture, and a Solution Concept Diagram to establish how the solution meets the objectives. In Phase B, create these artifacts: a Driver/Goal/Objective Catalog showing the flexibility of the solution across lines of business, a Business Service/Function Catalog to clarify governance and restrict unnecessary scope changes, and a Business Interaction Matrix for delineating communications among the various stakeholder teams.

C. In Phase A, create Stakeholder Map Matrix to clearly identify the stakeholders; in Phase B, create a Value Chain Diagram to establish the profitability of the solution, a Business Service/Function Catalog to show how the functional aspects of the solution satisfy business services, a Location Catalog to show—line-by-line—where each of the facilities are located and how far from each other they are, a Contract/Measure catalog to make sure everything in the contract is correctly measured against SLAs, and a Data Dissemination Diagram which will show how the data is shared among the various applications.

D. In Phase A, create the following artifacts: a Value Chain Diagram to give stakeholders an understanding of the overarching context of the architecture. In Phase B, select these artifacts: a Process/Event/Control/Product Diagram to show the cause and effect of the system in the solution, a Contract/Measure Catalog to clarify the service contracts and measures between the systems, an Actor/Role Matrix listing and cross-referencing people with processes, a Business Footprint Diagram to show the links between goals, organizations, functions, and services, and a Functional Decomposition Diagram.

SCENARIO #29 Matlock Gunsmiths

BACKGROUND

Matlock Gunsmiths is a 120 year-old manufacture of rifles, revolvers, pistols, and other lightweight personal defense weapons. They have a national presence with 4 manufacturing facilities each specializing in a particular class of weapons. Weapons manufacturers are bound by US government regulations and undergo periodic review of their compliance by the ATF. Recently, several competitors were found in violation of those regulations to some degree; one manufacturer was suspended from further weapons builds until it could prove compliance. Matlock hired a consultancy to simulate an ATF investigation and found several non-compliant issues: OSHA violations, shipping log discrepancies, security breaches, and loss of data due to theft and/or poor stewardship. This was in spite of documented and executed internal policies for DRBC, regular OSHA training classes, and an emphasis on security briefings.

The company's owners quickly moved on this information and fired 2 executive team leaders: the CTO and the COO. They replaced these with carefully chosen weapons manufacturing executives to overhaul the operations and technology architectures. The new executives were well versed in TOGAF® and immediately began working on re-architecting the enterprise. They hired 4 EA professionals: a Chief Architect, a Solutions Architect, a Transition Architect, and a Security Architect. Together with the stakeholders, they completed the Request for Architecture work and prepared for a cycle of the ADM.

During the final acceptance meeting, the CTO is most concerned about document security in light of recent leaks in other weapons manufacturers' facilities. She wants a detailed breakdown of how that aspect of the architecture being developed will address that concern.

QUESTION

Refer to the scenario

You are the Chief Architect and prepared a brief for the CTO to explain to her how the project will address her concerns. Based on TOGAF® 9, which of the following is the best answer to her concerns?

ANSWERS

A. Implement a BTEP so that all business units conduct a transformation readiness assessment to uncover business transformation security issues; perform NSA's DOCAS procedures; create a pseudo-security breach tool to test systems; conduct a Risk Assessment and combine it with a BTRA; qualify 3 teams for security intrusion protection and detection; determine readiness factors for success of the implementation; create a Consolidated Gaps, Solutions, and Dependencies Matrix to firmly fix the most critical security elements.

B. Gain a complete understanding of the business security requirements; find the pain point of the stakeholders for security constraints; obtain management support for security measures; determine and document applicable disaster recovery or business continuity plans/requirements; identify and document the anticipated physical/business/regulatory environment in which the system will be deployed. Determine "what can go wrong?"

C. Gain a complete understanding of the business security requirements; find the pain point of the stakeholders for security constraints; get a clear understanding of what assets need to be protected, from whom they need to be protected, who has authorization to access them and to what level of security they need; document security forensics, perform a threat analysis; and assess the impact of new security measures side effects. Determine "what can go wrong?"

D. Define and document applicable regulatory and security policy requirements; define the baseline current security-specific architecture elements; identify safe default actions and failure states; revisit assumptions regarding interconnecting systems beyond project control; identify the criticality of the availability and correct operation of each function; determine approaches to address identified risks; create an Implementation Factor Assessment and Deduction Matrix and Transition Architecture State Evolution Table. Determine "what can go wrong?"

SCENARIO #30 Perseus Rising Star

BACKGROUND

Perseus Rising Star (PRS) is a private-sector space technology enterprise, which just experienced an Initial Public Offer on the stock market. The results were better than they had expected and are now able to put to task tens of millions of dollars to break into full production mode. But before they can do that, they have to invest a good portion of that money in streamlining their operation. During the startup period, they were hiring the best of the best engineers from around the world to staff up a highly motivated and talented workforce. They had to give in to a plethora of technical software applications preferred by the new hires: they worked best with the tools that they knew and it would have been wasteful in time and money to impede progress toward their business goals.

Now, the advantages of allowing the engineers to use their own tools became a disadvantage. First, engineers hired later in the project would have to ramp up to learn the disparate tools of their seniors. Second, the projects that they were now beginning to run required modifications to the tools being used. The present applications would have to be scrapped or customized. In a meeting of the board, which also included the directors of the various engineering teams, there was made an agreement to scrap the old applications and purchase COTS software which would then be customized to fit the company's needs. Although not every team was satisfied with the choices made, all were in agreement to the plan.

PRS has had an Enterprise Architecture team since the founding of the company. EA principles are firmly entrenched so moving into an ADM cycle was a matter of routine. As the Statement of Architecture work was completed, the stakeholders needed to be ensured that the forklift changes to the applications used in the architecture will be carefully scrutinized so that business processes do not lose functionality and personnel do not lose the current cohesive inter-team communications they enjoy.

QUESTION

Refer to the scenario

You are the Chief Architect and will need to establish best practices for alleviating stakeholder concerns. Based on TOGAF® 9, which of the following is the best way to do that?

ANSWERS

A. In the first pass through the Architecture Development Iteration, create the following artifacts to establish the baseline architecture. In Phase B: an Organization/Actor Catalog, a Role Catalog, and a Business Use-Case Diagram; in Phase C (Data): an Application/Data Matrix, a Data Entity/Business Function Matrix, and a Data Entity/Data Component Catalog; in Phase C (Applications): an Application Use-Case Diagram, an Application/Function Matrix, a

Role/Application Matrix, and an Application/Organization Matrix. In Phase D: an Application/Technology Matrix. On the second pass, develop the target architecture and establish the gaps between baseline and target before moving on to Phase E.

B. In the first pass through the Architecture Development Iteration, create the following artifacts to establish the baseline architecture. In Phase B: an Application/Data Matrix, a Data Entity/Business Function Matrix, and a Data Entity/Data Component Catalog; in Phase C (Data): an Application Use-Case Diagram, an Application/Function Matrix, a Role/Application Matrix, and an Application/Organization Matrix; in Phase D: an Organization/Actor Catalog, a Role Catalog, and a Business Use-Case Diagram, and an Application/Technology Matrix. In the second pass, develop the target architecture and fill the gaps with transition architectures before moving on to Phase E.

C. In the first pass through the Architecture Development Iteration, create the following artifacts to establish the baseline architecture. In Phase B: an Organization/Actor Catalog, a Driver/Goal/Objective Catalog, and a Business Use-Case Diagram; in Phase C (Data): an Application/Data Matrix, a Data Entity/Business Function Matrix, and a Conceptual Data Diagram; in Phase C (Applications): an Interface Catalog, an Application/Function Matrix, a Role/Application Matrix, and an Application/Organization Matrix. In Phase D: an Application/Technology Matrix. On the second pass, develop the target architecture and establish the gaps between baseline and target before moving on to Phase E.

D. In the first pass through the Architecture Development Iteration, create the following artifacts to establish the baseline architecture. In Phase B: an Organization/Actor Catalog, a Role Catalog, and a Business Use-Case Diagram; in Phase C (Data): an Application/Data Matrix, a Data Entity/Business Function Matrix, and a Data Entity/Data Component Catalog; in Phase C (Applications): an Application Use-Case Diagram, an Application/Function Matrix, a Role/Application Matrix, and an Application/Organization Matrix; in Phase D: an Application/Technology Matrix. On the second pass, develop the target architecture and fill the gaps with transition architectures before moving on to Phase E.

SCENARIO #31 Protecture Security

BACKGROUND

Protecture Security is a provider of home and small business security solutions in 15 states, mainly in the Mid-Atlantic Region of the United States. Their reputation for service is strong as well as their financials. Home and small business security contracts have risen as a result of concerns along the eastern seaboard relating to reports of possible drug cartels setting up drop points for shipments of illegal narcotics to Europe. This rise in business has allowed Protecture to expand their product lines to include services for training and educating their customers on self-protection including self-defense classes and target practice. The expansion will require a new mind set for the company since direct one-on-one contact with the customer (aside from sales) has been minimal. The new vision requires transformation into a more extensive horizontal structure as it means hiring professional trainers, construction of self-defense facilities and gun ranges.

Protecture has engaged the services of an enterprise architecture-consulting firm located in Baltimore to oversee the transformation. They have confirmed governance and support frameworks, documented principles and tailored TOGAF® to meet the needs of the company. At the final meeting before the initiation of the ADM, the stakeholders laid out their concerns about the risks of transformation in the light of the cultural shift into the target solution. They want assurance that the company's lack of readiness does not impose a stumbling block to success, that their people are ready for the program, and that the systems are in place for transformation. They asked how the EA team would make sure these concerns were accounted for before proceeding with developing the new architecture.

QUESTION

Refer to the scenario

You are the Lead Architect assigned to prepare the EA team for execution of the Architecture Development Iteration.

Based on TOGAF® 9, which of the following is the best answer?

ANSWERS

A. In Phase A, determine the willingness of the disparate organizations in the enterprise to undergo the program, and that the vision is well understood. Ensure that there are stakeholders committed to watch over the progress of development and execution. Associate accountability with the appropriate stakeholders to specific areas of transformation. Classify risks in terms of time, budget, and scope. Establish the effect of risks in terms of catastrophic, critical, marginal, and negligible. Using that information, create a Risk Classification Scheme. Plan on the deployment of risk mitigation and asses the probable residual risks. Compile the results, review with the stakeholders, and document the final evaluation.

B. Present to the board that you expect that risks will be identified as a result of readiness assessments. The EA team will focus on areas that most affect continuity of service. They will watch for gaps that would preclude reaching interim transition points as well as reaching the final target architecture. Create a Risk Classification Matrix to classify risks according to the effect they will have, their expected frequency, and the level of risk for each. The solution will have built-in redundancies and fallbacks and the implementation will be closely watched using best practices-based review methods.

C. Determine the willingness of the disparate organizations in the enterprise to undergo the program, and that the vision is well understood. Ensure that there are stakeholders committed to watch over the progress of the development and execution. Associate accountability with the appropriate stakeholders to specific areas of transformation. Make sure that IT and the enterprise are capable of executing the plan and operating the solution after implementation. Summarize the urgency, status for readiness, and the cost of overcoming specific gaps. Compare the results with the risks involved. Compile the results, review with the stakeholders, and document the final evaluation.

D. In the Preliminary Phase classify risks in terms of time, budget, and scope. Ensure that there are shareholders committed to watch over the progress of the development and execution. Associate accountability with the appropriate stakeholders to specific areas of transformation. Use CMMs to help identify SBBs and ABBs imminent in the baseline and target architectures. Establish the effect of transitions in terms of catastrophic, critical, marginal, and negligible. Determine the exact frequency of the identified risks. Using that information, create a Risk Classification Scheme. The solution will have built-in redundancies and fallbacks and the implementation will be closely watched.

SCENARIO #32 Plinket Industries

BACKGROUND

Plinket Industries is a rail manufacturing company offering the most diversified rail industry product line available in North America. They are the leading producers in North America of freight cars, tank cars, railcar axles, and coupling devices. They manufacture a full line of freight cars, including covered and open hoppers, gondolas, auto carriers, boxcars, and intermodal cars. They also produce a full line of tank cars that transport liquefied and pressurized commodities.

Plinket is very dependent on CAD engineers for designing and engineering new products. The Product Development team has been on the cutting edge of their field due to highly experienced staff and their industry-recognized VP of Products. They are given carte blanche in purchasing the most sophisticated applications to keep them leaders in the industry.

The Information Technology organization, however, has not been able to keep up with the growth of application demands on the network and hardware systems, other than the workstations used by the PD team. Budgeting, outside of product development has been targeted more toward logistics. Recently, the VP of Products and VP of Information Technology met with the CFO to explain that by not upgrading the aging IT infrastructure, the PD team will begin to lose the ability to grow. The systems will meet their physical limitations. The CFO agreed and contracted with an enterprise architecture consultancy to upgrade the systems. The executives met with the Chief Enterprise Architect to begin the planning for the new architecture.

The VPs of Product and IT expressed their concern that since the applications and data used by the company have been running on the aging technology infrastructure, that the new hardware platforms and, especially, operating systems will be the right fit: scalable, but not overbuilt for the functions needed. They want to be involved in reviews at each phase transition with the authority to modify or veto any aspect of the development of the Target Architecture, especially where the underlying systems are concerned.

QUESTION

Refer to the scenario

Based on TOGAF® 9, which of the following is the best approach to satisfy their needs?

ANSWERS

A. Establish milestones for conducting Compliance Reviews between each phase of the ADM cycle focusing on the deliverables for the Draft Architecture Definition Documents in the Architecture Development iterations. The Technology Architecture Phase will receive special attention to ensure that the new technology platforms will service the needs of the Business, Data, and Application Architectures. After Phase E, a milestone meeting will concentrate on the deliverables for Transition Architecture and the Architecture Roadmap to provide assurance that the Migration and Planning Phase will have a solid basis for creating the Migration and Implementation Plan. The Compliance Review after Phase F will involve all major stakeholders to provide a chance for re-architecting should the stakeholders not concur with the Architecture Board's decision to proceed. Compliance Reviews will be held throughout the Implementation and Governance Phase and Architecture Change Management Phases for additional adjustments to the Target Architecture.

B. Establish milestones for conducting Compliance Reviews between each phase of the ADM cycle focusing on the deliverables for the Draft Architecture Definition Documents in the Architecture Development iterations. The Technology Architecture Phase will receive special attention to ensure that the new technology platforms will service the needs of the Business Architecture. After Phase E, a milestone meeting will concentrate on the deliverables for Transition Architecture and the Architecture Roadmap to provide assurance that the Migration and Planning Phase will have a solid basis for creating the Migration and Implementation Plan. The Compliance Review after Phase F will involve all major stakeholders to provide a chance for re-architecting should the stakeholders not concur with the Architecture Board's decision to proceed. Further Compliance Reviews will be held during Requirements Management but are not performed in Phases G and H since no major changes will be allowed to occur.

C. Establish milestones for conducting Compliance Reviews during the Preliminary Phase. Hold the next review at the end of the first and second iterations of the Architecture Development Iteration focusing on the deliverables for the Draft Architecture Definition Documents. The Technology Architecture Phase will receive special attention to ensure that the new technology platforms will service the needs of the Business, Data, and Application Architectures. After Phase F, a milestone meeting will concentrate on the deliverables for Transition Architecture and the Architecture Roadmap to provide assurance that the Migration and Planning Phase will have a solid basis for creating the Migration and Implementation Plan. The Compliance Review after Phase F will involve all major stakeholders to provide a chance for re-architecting should the stakeholders not concur with the Architecture Board's decision to proceed. Further Compliance Reviews will be held during Requirements Management but are not performed in Phases G and H since no major changes will be allowed to occur.

D. Establish milestones for conducting Compliance Reviews using the format shown in the Requirements Management Phase and focusing on the deliverables for the Draft Architecture Definition Documents. The Technology Architecture Phase will include the Network/Data/Application Diagram and Business/Function Diagram. New technology platforms will service the needs of the Business, Data, and Application Architectures. After Phase G, a milestone meeting will concentrate on the deliverables for Transition Architecture and the Architecture Roadmap to provide assurance that the Statement of Architecture Work will have a solid basis for creating the Migration and Implementation Plan. The Compliance Review after Phase H will involve all major stakeholders to provide a chance for re-architecting should the stakeholders not concur with the Architecture Board's decision to proceed. Compliance Reviews will be held throughout the Implementation and Governance Phase and Architecture Change Management Phases for additional adjustments to the Target Architecture.

SCENARIO SET #4 ANSWER KEYS

SCENARIO #25 Amsterdam Chemical

Topic		Architecture Deliverable
Subjects/Rationale		The scenario requires the student to understand how architecture deliverables are used in TOGAF®
Most Correct	D	Each of these deliverables will provide the stakeholders with the best information related to their concerns
Second Best	B	The Capability Assessment and Value Chain Diagram are not directly relevant
Third Best	C	The Organizational Model for Enterprise Architecture is not directly relevant, neither are the Architecture Repository, Architecture Governance Framework, or Principles Catalog
Distractor	A	There are many issues with this answer.

SCENARIO #26 Forth-Write Construction

Topic		Capability-Based Planning
Subjects/Rationale		The scenario asks for details on how to conduct Capability-Based Planning
Most Correct	C	This answer summarizes the information in section 32.4 (see figure 32-4)
Second Best	B	The Phases and Transition Iteration are incorrect
Third Best	D	Although the BTRA and the Gap Analysis may be referenced, are not directly related to Capability-Based Planning. The Preliminary Phase reference is incorrect.
Distractor	A	Fundamentally incorrect.

SCENARIO #27 GB Hospitals

Topic	Interoperability	
Subjects/Rationale	This scenario focuses on establishing interoperability of the solution components	
Most Correct	C	This answer follows the guidelines in TOGAF® to approach interoperability evaluation in terms of information exchange.
Second Best	B	An Implementation Factor Assessment and Deduction Matrix is not a valid tool for this task.
Third Best	D	The BTRA is not relevant. The Gap Analysis is required but is outside the scope of the task. The Transition Architecture State Evolution Table is not a valid tool for this task.
Distractor	A	Several elements of this answer are from disparate parts of the TOGAF® model not relating to interoperability.

SCENARIO #28 Lone Star Beans, Inc.

Topic	Artifacts	
Subjects/Rationale	Correctly selecting the appropriate artifacts for a solution	
Most Correct	B	These artifacts satisfy the concerns of the stakeholders by giving a clear view of the services and functions and their interactions.
Second Best	A	This choice has some of the correct artifacts but incorrectly includes artifacts focused on people rather than the immediate concern about functions.
Third Best	D	This answer barely satisfies the concerns of the stakeholders and provides some unrelated artifacts.
Distractor	C	Misplaced artifacts, misunderstood artifacts, and unrelated artifacts.

SCENARIO #29 Matlock Gunsmiths

Topic		Security and the ADM
Subjects/Rationale		The scenarios asks for steps involved in addressing security architecture in the ADM
Most Correct	C	These answers provide the best answer to approach the concerns of the stakeholders
Second Best	B	Many of the answers are correct, but many of them are already in place.
Third Best	D	More answers that are not relevant to the concerns
Distractor	A	Completely wrong.

SCENARIO #30 Perseus Rising Star

Topic		Artifacts
Subjects/Rationale		The scenario requires knowledge of usage of artifacts
Most Correct	A	The artifacts chosen here address the concerns of the stakeholders involving application consolidation
Second Best	C	The Driver/Goal/Objective Catalog, Conceptual Data Diagram, and Interface Catalog do not fully address the concerns.
Third Best	D	Filling gaps and creating transition architectures are performed later in the ADM
Distractor	B	The right artifacts in the wrong phases

SCENARIO #31 Protecture Security

Topic		Business Transformation Readiness Assessment
Subjects/Rationale		The scenario requires the completion of the BTRA
Most Correct	C	This is the complete solution as it describes the process of the Business Transformation Readiness Assessment
Second Best	A	This answer is partially true, but leaves out many BTRA tasks and adds Risk Management tasks, which are separate.
Third Best	B	This is purely Risk Management, which my satisfy some of the requirements, but is not on the mark.
Distractor	D	This answer is a combination of incorrect substance from several methods.

SCENARIO #32 Plinket Industries

Topic		Architecture Compliance
Subjects/Rationale		Insure that the architecture is compliant with the target goals
Most Correct	A	Follows the Guidelines set in the Architecture Compliance section of TOGAF®
Second Best	B	Compliance Reviews are not held in the Requirements Phase but will always be held in Phases G and H.
Third Best	C	Milestones are not set in the Preliminary Phase; Compliance Reviews should be held at the end of each phase, not just after an iteration cycle; the first mention of Phase F should actually describe what happens in Phase E. Compliance Reviews are not held in the Requirements Phase but will always be held in Phases G and H.
Distractor	D	Wrong Phases, documents, deliverables

Set 5: Scenarios 33-40

SCENARIO #33 Elegant Solutions 4 U

BACKGROUND

Elegant Solutions 4 U (ES4U) is a relatively young software development enterprise specializing in producing sub-programs for the growing electronic gaming industry. It is a small company with only 150 programmer/analysts and a small executive staff. It does, however, produce 87% of sub-programs used their clients. Their sales team is an aggressive group of individuals who must keep the sales funnel filled since most contracts are as little as three weeks long. For each customer they may have 10-20 separate live contracts at a time, and they have to be vigilant for new opportunities.

The ES4U "cold" sales team brought in a contract with a new firm which would provide a steady stream of contracts equaling the average of the sum of the existing customer contracts. The executive staff and lead technologist were at first adverse to the relationship, however, because the potential client was in a completely different market: writing applications for convenience stores. This meant a change in the business plan and caused considerable concern with ES4U investors. In the end, though, the major shareholders agreed to a plan that would essentially create a separate entity to test the idea of expanding the business mission statement. If successful, they would consider an overhaul of the corporation to serve a larger market.

As the executives and directors began evaluating the changes required, they first considered the addition of 25 new developers into the company. Since the new business unit would be functionally separate from the existing one, there was some disagreement on usage of assets. Some were adamant that they purchase an entirely new technology infrastructure since they considered the new hires to be a potential security threat, especially if the experiment was a failure resulting in a loss of their jobs. The IT Director, however, sided with the CFO by affirming that, with new security policies, that threat would be greatly diminished; that the cost of new assets would be more than a breach of security. The final meeting resulted in following the CFO and IT Director's recommendations.

QUESTION

Refer to the scenario

You are the IT Director and an expert in TOGAF® methodologies. Based on TOGAF® 9, which of the following is the best way to ensure that the shareholders' concerns are addressed?

ANSWERS

A. Create a new security policy by directing the Solutions Architect to create a Data and Information Asset Disposition Catalog after an audit of the IT organization's systems. Then conduct a risk assessment to classify and identify potential security risks, and produce a Risk Identification and Mitigation Assessment Worksheet. Initiate an iteration of Requirements Management and based on the updated security requirements, produce and announce a new official security policy. Create a Codified Data/Information Asset Ownership and Custody Catalog. Conduct an iteration of Phase H to revise change management guidelines using the resulting documentation and a Data Classification Policy Catalog.

B. Create a new security policy by directing the Solutions Architect to create an Application/Technology Matrix after an audit of the IT organization's systems. Use a Business Value Assessment Technique to prove the cost/benefit of the change, and then produce a Risk Identification and Mitigation Assessment Worksheet. Initiate an iteration of Phase G. Based on the updated security requirements, produce and announce a new official security policy. Create a Codified Data/Information Asset Ownership and Custody Catalog. Conduct an iteration of Phase H to revise change management guidelines using the resulting documentation and a Data Entity/Data Component Catalog.

C. Begin a revision of existing security policies by directing the Solutions Architect to create a Data and Information Asset Disposition Catalog after an audit of the IT organization's systems. Then conduct a risk assessment to classify and identify potential security risks, and produce a Risk Identification and Mitigation Assessment Worksheet. Use Requirements Management to update security requirements and produce and announce a new official security policy. Create a Codified Data/Information Asset Ownership and Custody Catalog. Conduct an iteration of Phase H to revise change management guidelines using the resulting documentation and a Data Classification Policy Catalog.

D. Begin a revision of existing security policies by directing the Solutions Architect to create a Data and Security Asset Disposition Catalog after an audit of each of the Business Units. Then conduct a risk value and authority assessment to eliminate potential security risks; produce a Risk Authority and Access Assessment Worksheet. Initiate an iteration of the Architecture Development Iteration. In Phases E-F, based on the updated security requirements, produce and announce a new official security policy. Create a Custody Catalog and Security Validation/Risk Identification Catalog, Matrix, and Diagram. Conduct an iteration of Phase G to revise change management guidelines using the resulting documentation and a Data Classification Policy Catalog.

SCENARIO #34 Basis Computers

BACKGROUND

Basis Computers has had a remarkable rise in the retail PC manufacturing and on-line sales market. In 5 years, it has grown from 5 employees to 1,000 from an annual income of $50,000 to over $670 million. It has a very aggressive sales force and, fortunately, a finely tuned manufacturing and logistical system. The growth, however, has recently hit a wall. It looks as if the revenue gains have leveled off and have had a slight downturn. The executive staff has been examining all offices and teams to find the source of the losses. They have eliminated all but the most important travel, put all training on hold, and cut down on normal office expenditures. Last month, they reduced their workforce by 10%. The investors have finally met with the CEO and CFO and told them that they must find a way to reverse the negative flow or be replaced.

The two executives heard about the concept of Enterprise Architecture at a recent conference and had exchanged business cards with one of the EA consultancy experts. The CEO called a meeting with the firm to get more information on this concept. Once he understood the principles, he made a visit to the CFO to confirm and agree that they should move forward with hiring the EA consultant. After convincing the investors to allow them to try this venture, they immediately called in the EA channel team to evaluate their enterprise.

They spent a great deal of time talking to stakeholders, establishing the scope, looking at governance frameworks, and getting a grasp on the company's capabilities. They determined that these issues were the roots of the problem: Enterprise architecture processes, documentation, and standards were established by a variety of ad hoc means and are localized or informal. There was minimal linkage to business strategies and business drivers. Little communication existed about the enterprise architecture process and possible process improvements.

They presented their report to the CEO, CFO and shareholders. The two majority shareholders were skeptical and wanted an explanation of how the EA teams would solve these problems.

QUESTION

Refer to the scenario

You are the Chief Architect. Based on TOGAF® 9, which of the following is the best answer?

ANSWERS

    A. In Phase A, use business scenarios to uncover information and service exchanges as they exist today. Begin the first iteration of the Architecture Development Phase to establish the Baseline Architecture. In Phase B, define the information and service exchanges in business terms. In Phase C—Data Architecture, using the corporate data and/or information exchange model, detail the content of the information exchanges. In Phase C—Application Architecture, specify how the various applications share information and services. In Phase D, specify the technical mechanisms that are failing to permit the information and service exchanges. On the second iteration, in developing the Target Architecture, review the deliverables from Phases B-D and create a framework to replace the current environment. After Target development, in Phase E, identify the gaps and select the actual solutions. In Phase F, implement the new interoperable system.

B. Begin the first iteration of the Architecture Development Phase to establish the Baseline Architecture. In Phase B, use business scenarios to uncover information and service exchanges as they exist today, and define them in business terms. In Phase C—Data Architecture, using the corporate data and/or information exchange model, detail the content of the information exchanges. In Phase C—Application Architecture, specify how the various applications share information and services. In Phase D, specify the technical mechanisms that are failing to permit the information and service exchanges. On the second iteration, in developing the Target Architecture, review the deliverables from Phases B-D and create a framework to replace the current environment. After Target development, in Phase E, and select the actual solutions. In Phase F, implement the new interoperable system.

C. In Phase A, use business scenarios to uncover information and service exchanges as they exist today. You decide not to establish the Baseline Architecture with the intent to implement a greenfield architecture. Begin the Architecture Development Phase to establish the Target Architecture. In Phase B, define the information and service exchanges in business terms. In Phase C—Data Architecture, using the corporate data and/or information exchange model, detail the content of the information exchanges. In Phase C—Application Architecture, specify how the various applications share information and services. In Phase D, specify the appropriate technical mechanisms to permit information and service exchanges. In Phase E, identify the gaps and select the actual solutions. In Phase F, implement the new interoperable system.

D. Use business scenarios to determine information and service exchange considerations. Further define them in business terms. Determine the content of the information exchanges, how applications are to be shared, and the appropriate technical mechanisms that will enable the flow of information. Refine the information exchange plan in terms of degrees, types, and strategic targets and then update the gap analysis. Determine information exchange requirements using a Business Operation Interoperability Matrix and an

Implementation Factor Assessment and Deduction Matrix to reconcile the information exchange requirements with potential solutions. Select the solutions that will facilitate the exchanges and build them into the interoperability plan for implementation.

SCENARIO #35 SASSI

BACKGROUND

SASSI (Sweet as Sugar Sweeteners, Inc.) is a producer and distributor of artificial sweeteners, as well as diabetes-safe candies: Sassy Bites. Sassy Bites had a faster-than-expected growth rate and moved out of its test market in Indiana into three other states. I was such a big success that SASSI decided to move ahead with a nationwide distribution. This decision is tightly coupled with a need to build two candy factories, one in Charlotte, NC, for the Eastern US, and one in Dallas, TX, for the West. SASSI will also establish a Sassy Bites head office with oversight of its own President in Dallas, led by the recently promoted VP of Product Marketing.

The existing enterprise architecture is fairly well established, as it was created using solid TOGAF® principles. However, the expansion and organizational change is expected to be very risky. The Baseline Architecture is stable and, for the most part, not in need of any new development. But the architectural framework for Sassy Bites needs to be approached without a prejudice for using the existing framework for the rest of SASSI.

Because of this, the stakeholders are concerned that, to the extent possible, all risks should be carefully examined and contingencies set. Product Development added another concern that the information systems would be secure from data loss as well as possible security breaches during the transition. They also were wary of the theft of intellectual property (e.g., recipes) being threatened since the factory in Indianapolis will be shut down—potentially causing employee abuse—and new personnel in the new facilities that will not have established trust and loyalty to the company.

QUESTION

Refer to the scenario

SASSI has an experienced NA team with you as the Chief Architect. Based on TOGAF® 9, which of the following is the best way to address these concerns?

ANSWERS

A. Begin a review of existing management policies found in the Enterprise Continuum Repositories. If necessary, based on the updated asset requirements, produce and announce a new official procurement policy. In the Preliminary Phase, classify risks in terms of time, budget, and scope. Use CMMs to help identify risks imminent in the baseline and target architectures. Establish the effect of risks in terms of catastrophic, critical, marginal, and negligible. Determine the expected frequency of the identified risks. Using that information, create a Risk Classification Matrix to classify risks according to the effect they will have, their expected frequency, and the level of risk for each. Plan on the deployment of risk mitigation and asses the probable residual risks. Through a series of interviews, document the expectations of the stakeholders to assess business risks; account for stakeholder limits on risk mitigation; identify the assets that need to be retained, which need to be replaced, who has authorization to audit them and purchase them. The solution will have built-in redundancies and fallbacks and the implementation will be closely watched using best practices based review methods.

B. Initiate an iteration of Requirements Management and begin a review of existing security policies found in the Enterprise Continuum Repositories. If necessary, based on the updated security requirements, produce and announce a new official security policy. In Phase A, classify risks in terms of time, budget, and scope. Use CMMs to help identify risks imminent in the baseline and target architectures. Establish the effect of risks in terms of catastrophic, critical, marginal, and negligible. Determine the expected frequency of the identified risks. Using that information, create a Risk Classification Scheme. Plan on the deployment of risk mitigation and asses the probable residual risks. Through a series of interviews, document the expectations of the stakeholders to assess business security requirements; account for stakeholder limits on security constraints; identify the assets that need to be protected, from whom they need to be protected, who has authorization to access them and to what level of security they need; document security forensics, perform a threat analysis; and assess the impact of new security measures side effects.

C. Begin with the Technology Phase and identify gaps in the current technology infrastructure to meet the demands of new manufacturing constraints; then update the Technology Portfolio Catalog, the Application/Technology Matrix, Platform Description Diagram, and Network Computing Hardware Diagram to document additions and changes to fill the gaps in the Technology Architecture. Follow this with a pass through the Application Architecture with a gap analysis to determine any deficiencies in the applications to perform possible new functions; update the Application Portfolio, Interface Catalog, Application Interaction Matrix, and Application Use-Case Diagram. Then perform an iteration of the Data Architecture, first identifying possible gaps in the current design to fulfill the needs of the new architecture; update the Application/Data Matrix, and the Logical Data Diagram as needed. Last, execute an iteration of the Business Architecture, first conducting a gap analysis to see what business processes will be affected; update the Business Service/Function Catalog, the Process/Event/Control/Product Catalog, and the Goal/Objective/Service Diagram.

D. Gain a complete understanding of and assess the business security requirements; find the pain point of the stakeholders for security constraints; get a clear understanding of what assets need to be protected, and from whom they need to be protected, who has authorization to access them and to what level of security they need; document security forensics, perform a threat analysis; and assess the impact of new security measures side effects; determine "what can go wrong?" Begin a revision of existing security policies by directing the Solutions Architect to create a Data and Information Asset Disposition Catalog after an audit of the IT organization's systems. Then conduct a risk assessment to classify and identify potential security risks, and produce a Risk Identification and Mitigation Assessment Worksheet. Initiate an iteration of Requirements Management and based on the updated security requirements, produce and announce a new official security policy. Create a Codified Data/Information Asset Ownership and Custody Catalog. Conduct an iteration of Phase H to revise change management guidelines using the resulting documentation and a Data Classification Policy Catalog.

SCENARIO #36 Creature Comforts Hospitality

BACKGROUND

Creature Comforts Hospitality (CCH) holds a chain of 690 hotels in 17 southern and mid-western states. They have experienced a slow but steady growth rate, having only one negative balance quarter in its 5-year history. They have approached increasing their market by building new hotels, refurbishing and redesigning hotels obtained through real estate deals, and have a handful of facilities that are not branded, but owned by the company.

CCH hired a new CIO to review and report on the state of the IT infrastructure of the company. He found that there was a significant amount of duplicated processes, redundant independent data stores, application version inconsistencies, and outdated network and hardware systems. There was a major security problem, which, in several cases, allowed employees access to sensitive information that was being sold to competitors. He recommended a complete overhaul, keeping within budgetary constraints. He also recommended that they hire permanent staff of enterprise architects with certification and experience in TOGAF® 9. He had had positive experience with a team in his last company and requested new billets be opened to bring them on.

The executive staff agreed, but wanted to be informed at every step of the transition from requirements gathering to operational status. They were clear that the project was not to begin until they had established close communications with the EAs. The CIO, after the new hires were brought on board, briefed the Chief Architect on the functional and political situation at CCH. He wanted to know how the transition plan would address stakeholder concerns.

QUESTION

Refer to the scenario

You are the Chief Architect. Based on TOGAF® 9, which of the following is the best answer?

ANSWERS

A. In the Preliminary Phase, identify the key players in the engagement. Using artifacts from the Enterprise Continuum, conduct an iteration of Requirements Management to re-use previously successful stakeholder analysis matrices. Also pull different views of the business, information system, and technology architectures. In Phase A, determine whom the main executive stakeholders are, concentrating on the established hierarchy of the company's organization. In Phase B, produce a Stakeholder Analysis matrix and classify stakeholder requirements. Determine the stakeholder management approach used within the customer's baseline framework. Create Stakeholder Map identifying the key players, the ones to keep satisfied, and the ones to keep informed.

B. In the Preliminary Phase, while scoping the enterprise organizations impacted, create a Stakeholder Map identifying the key players, the ones to keep satisfied, and the ones to keep informed. In Phase A, create different views of the business, information system, and technology architectures. Determine who the main enterprise architecture stakeholders are, including informal stakeholder groups. Identify and catalog which stakeholders belong to more than one stakeholder group. Produce a Stakeholder Analysis matrix and classify stakeholder positions. Determine the stakeholder management approach. Identify catalogs, matrices, and diagrams that the architecture engagement needs to produce and validate with each stakeholder group to deliver an effective architecture model.

C. In the Preliminary Phase, while scoping the enterprise organizations impacted, create a Stakeholder Map identifying the key players, the ones to keep satisfied, and the ones to keep informed. Determine the stakeholder management approach. Determine who the main enterprise architecture stakeholders are, including informal stakeholder groups. Create a Value Chain Diagram and Solution Concept Diagram to review with the stakeholders. In Phase A, Identify catalogs, matrices, and diagrams that the architecture engagement needs to produce and validate with each stakeholder group to deliver an effective architecture model. Classify stakeholder positions. In Phase B, write an Organization/Actor Catalog, a Role Catalog, a Business Interaction Matrix, and Actor/ Role Matrix.

D. In Phase A, create Stakeholder Map identifying the key players, the ones to keep satisfied and the ones to keep informed. Create different views of the business, information system, and technology architectures. Determine who the main enterprise architecture stakeholders are, including informal stakeholder groups. Identify and catalog which stakeholders belong to more than one stakeholder group. Produce a Stakeholder Analysis matrix and classify stakeholder positions. Determine the stakeholder management approach. Build a Stakeholder Power Grid. Identify catalogs, matrices, and diagrams that the architecture engagement needs to produce and validate with each stakeholder group to deliver an effective architecture model.

SCENARIO #37 Bernadi Auto Veloci #1

BACKGROUND

Bernadi Auto Veloci is an Italian sports car manufacturer based in Napoli, Italy. Founded by Marco Bernadi in 1947, the company sponsored drivers and manufactured racecars before moving into production of street-legal vehicles. Throughout its history, the company has been noted for its continued participation in racing, especially in Formula One, where it has had great success. Bernadi road cars are generally seen as a symbol of luxury and wealth. Bernadi has an internally managed merchandising line that licenses many products bearing the Bernadi brand, including eyewear, pens, pencils, electronic goods, perfume, cologne, clothing, high-tech bicycles, watches, cell phones, and even laptop computers.

The CIO has, after several sessions with the Network and Computing division of the Manufacturing business unit, approached the CEO and CFO about upgrading the technology support systems and also to re-configure the technology architecture of the company. All three of them had recently attended a conference in Napoli on Enterprise Architecture Featuring TOGAF® and were impressed with the presentation as well as the success stories of companies that instituted it. They felt that this task would be a good way to introduce themselves into the TOGAF® model. Because they were not experienced in EA, they hired a consultancy to provide the leadership of the transition, and to train select employees to take over the responsibility in later projects.

The systems engineers were concerned with ensuring that the appropriate components are developed and deployed within the system in an optimal manner and expressed that the concern be addressed in the program.

QUESTION

Refer to the scenario

You are the Chief Architect from the consultancy. Based on TOGAF® 9, which of the following is the best way to address these concerns?

ANSWERS

    A. In each phase of the first iteration of the Architecture Development iteration select reference models, viewpoints, and tools; develop baseline architecture description; and create a gap analysis matrix filling the baseline axis with the services in place in both of the enterprises' architecture. In the second iteration, develop the target architecture and enumerate the gap analysis matrix with the target services listed along the target services axis. Document the gaps between the two architectures; define candidate roadmap components resolve impacts across the Architecture Landscape; conduct formal stakeholder review; and finalize the architecture.

B. Focus on hardware, software, and networking. Determine the optimal locations of the systems and that they are designed for easy modification and re-usability. Ensure the availability of all components of the system with a comprehensive design including redundancy, availability, and reliability. Design application components to be assembled into a working, siloed system. Evaluate technology, which already exists in the organization, and what is available currently or in the near future. Finally, design the system so that appropriate components are developed and deployed within the system in an optimal manner.

C. Focus on hardware, software, and networking. Determine the optimal locations of the systems and that they are designed for easy modification and re-usability. Ensure the availability of all components of the system with a comprehensive design including redundancy, availability, and reliability. Design software and hardware components to be assembled into a working, holistic system. Evaluate technology, which already exists in the organization, and what is available currently or in the near future. Finally, design the system so that appropriate components are developed and deployed within the system in an optimal manner.

D. Focus on hardware, software, and networking. Determine the optimal locations of the systems and that they are designed for easy modification and re-usability. Ensure the availability of all components of the system with a comprehensive design including redundancy, availability, and reliability. Design the system so that appropriate components are developed and deployed within the system in an optimal manner. In the Technology Architecture Phase, create a Technology Portfolio Catalog, an Application/Technology Matrix, a Platform Composition Diagram, a Networked/Computing Hardware Diagram, and Communications Engineering Plan.

SCENARIO #38 Bernadi Auto Veloci #2

BACKGROUND

Bernadi Auto Veloci is an Italian sports car manufacturer based in Napoli, Italy. Founded by Marco Bernadi in 1947, the company sponsored drivers and manufactured racecars before moving into production of street-legal vehicles. Throughout its history, the company has been noted for its continued participation in racing, especially in Formula One, where it has had great success. Bernadi road cars are generally seen as a symbol of luxury and wealth. Bernadi has an internally managed merchandising line that licenses many products bearing the Bernadi brand, including eyewear, pens, pencils, electronic goods, perfume, cologne, clothing, high-tech bicycles, watches, cell phones, and even laptop computers.

Bernadi's CIO has requested an overhaul of their application development division. Over the past year, the company transformed its technology subsystems into state-of-the-art network and computing systems. Software applications were not considered as part of the program. The software developers had consistently produced well-crafted applications but they believe that if they were provided the same level of development tools, they would be able to expand their capabilities and actually provide the company with advanced CAD techniques that would take the R&D team to the next level.

The CFO and CEO agreed to the request and put their in-house EA team on the task. Since they had successfully completed the technology transition, they felt that they would be able to execute this upgrade as well. However, the CIO also wanted to ensure that the Target Application Architecture was thoroughly vetted to insure interoperability, portability, and flexibility.

QUESTION

Refer to the scenario

You are the Lead Enterprise Architect. Based on TOGAF® 9, which of the following is the best way to address the CIO's concerns?

ANSWERS

A. Evaluate the current software applications that support modularity and re-use to promote a flexible and efficient software development foundation. Link that review with an examination of software portability. Ensure that each software element is ready for migration and will interoperate between them. Assess information-intensive software to see if it provides the necessary views for stakeholder consumption as well as removing views that are not going to be necessary for the Target Architecture. Last, establish transparency in these areas: access, failure, location, migration, relocation, replication, and transactions.

B. Evaluate the current software applications that support mobility and presence to promote a flexible and efficient software development foundation. Link that review with an examination of software diversity. Ensure that each software element is ready for migration and will interoperate between them. Assess information-intensive software to see if it provides the necessary views for stakeholder consumption as well as removing views that are not going to be necessary from the Baseline Architecture. Last, establish opacity in these areas: access, failure, location, migration, relocation, replication, and transactions.

C. Evaluate the current software applications that support modularity and re-use to promote a flexible and efficient software development foundation. Link that review with an examination of software portability. Ensure that each software element is ready for migration and will interoperate between them. Assess information-intensive software to see if it provides the necessary views for stakeholder consumption as well as removing views that are not going to be necessary for the Target Architecture. In the Application Architecture Phase, create an Application Portfolio Catalog, a Role/Application Interface Matrix, an Applications Communications Diagram, and a Software Engineering Diagram.

D. Use Business Scenarios to analyze the existing environment and the requirements and constraints affecting the new system. Evaluate existing internal specifications and lists of approved products, business goals and objectives, business process re-engineering activities, and changes in technology. Evaluate the ease-of-use of the user interface, and how intuitive it is. Determine whether or not there is transparent access to data and applications, irrespective of location. Ensure: ease-of-management of the user environment by the user; application interoperability through means such as drag-and-drop; online help facilities; clarity of documentation; and security and password aspects.

SCENARIO #39 Hannitz/Colmburg Fashions #1

BACKGROUND

Hannitz/Colmburg Fashions (H/CF) is a retail-clothing company, known for its 2nd tier fashion clothing for men, women, teenagers and children. It has over 1,300 stores in 10 countries and as of 2011 employed around 14,000 people. It is ranked the fifteenth largest global clothing retailer. The design team in the company's Slovakia office controls the steps of production from merchandise planning to establishing specifications, and production is outsourced to approximately 50 factories in Europe and Latin America. These facilities are used for horizontal division of labor rather than being integrated.

H/CF will soon acquire three other similar fashion chains as their earnings over the past year have increased substantially. They will phase in the acquisitions sequentially over a period of three years. Their first buy will be Yakovich clothing in Bosnia-Herzegovina. It is the smallest of the three with just 5 stores and 1 production factory in Nuem on the coast of the Adriatic Sea.

H/CF has a mature Enterprise Architecture team that has been in existence for 4 years and has performed many successful projects using the TOGAF® model. But this will be the first time that they have attempted a merging of a new entity into the enterprise. One of the concerns of the stakeholders is the state of Yakovich's Business Architecture. They are unsure of their approach to business processes, people, and functions; whether their information flows, usability of systems and performance match those of H/CF.

The stakeholders have invited the Lead Enterprise Architect to hear how the program will address this concern.

QUESTION

Refer to the scenario

You are the Lead EA. Based on TOGAF® 9, which of the following is the best answer?

ANSWERS

A. In the Preliminary Phase, identify the key players in the engagement. Using artifacts from the Enterprise Continuum, conduct an iteration of Requirements Management to re-use previously successful stakeholder analysis matrices. Pull different views of the business, information system, and technology architectures. In Phase A, determine whom the main executive stakeholders are, concentrating on the established hierarchy of the company's organization. In Phase B, produce a Stakeholder Analysis matrix and classify stakeholder requirements. Determine the stakeholder management approach used within the customer's baseline framework. Create Stakeholder Map identifying the key players, the ones to keep satisfied, and the ones to keep informed. Ensure user-friendly systems using a Role/Application Matrix. An Application Interaction Matrix, Application Communication Diagram, Application and User Location Diagram, and Application Use-Case Diagram will also support user functions.

B. Get a clear understanding of the functional requirements for the new architecture. Develop Business Scenarios analyzing the existing environment and the requirements and constraints affecting the new system. Evaluate existing internal specifications and lists of approved products, business goals and objectives, business process re-engineering activities, and changes in technology. Consider concerns about people, processes, functions, business information, usability, and performance. Evaluate the ease-of-use of the user interface. Determine whether or not there is transparent access to data and applications, irrespective of location. Determine ease-of-management of the user environment by the user; application interoperability through means such as drag-and-drop; online help facilities; clarity of documentation; security and password aspects, such as avoiding the requirement for multiple sign-on and password dialogs; and access to productivity applications.

C. In the Preliminary Phase get a clear understanding of the data, application, and technical functional requirements for the new architecture. Develop Business Scenarios analyzing the existing environment and considering requirements for the target architecture. Evaluate existing application and data specifications and lists of approved products, process goals and objectives, business process re-engineering activities, and changes in application usage. Consider concerns about data entry, processes, hardware, security, and functionality. Conduct a Cost-Benefit analysis. Create a Business Footprint Diagram, a Business Interaction Matrix, and an Application/Role/Data Matrix. Document process requirements with a Process/Application Realization Diagram. Ensure user-friendly systems using a Role/Application Matrix. An Application Interaction Matrix, Application Communication Diagram, Application and User Location Diagram, and Application Use-Case Diagram.

D. Get a clear understanding of the technical requirements for the new architecture. Develop Business Scenarios analyzing the existing data and application environments and the requirements and constraints affecting the new system. Evaluate existing internal specifications and lists of approved products, business goals and objectives, business process re-engineering activities, and changes in technology. Consider concerns about data, processes, functions, security, usability, and performance. Evaluate the modular aspects of the user interface, and how intuitive it is. Determine whether or not there is transparent access to data and applications, irrespective of location. Determine the ease-of-management of the user environment; application interoperability through means such as drag-and-drop; online help facilities; clarity of documentation; security and password aspects, such as avoiding the requirement for multiple sign-on and password dialogs; and access to productivity applications.

SCENARIO #40 Hannitz/Colmburg Fashions #2

BACKGROUND

Hannitz/Colmburg Fashions (H/CF) is a retail-clothing company, known for its 2nd tier fashion clothing for men, women, teenagers and children. It has over 1,300 stores in 10 countries and as of 2011 employed around 14,000 people. It is ranked the fifteenth largest global clothing retailer. The design team in the company's Slovakia office controls the steps of production from merchandise planning to establishing specifications, and production is outsourced to approximately 50 factories in Europe and Latin America. These facilities are used for horizontal division of labor rather than being integrated.

H/CF will soon acquire three other similar fashion chains as their earnings over the past year have increased substantially. They will phase in the acquisitions sequentially over a period of three years. Their first buy will be Yakovich clothing in Bosnia-Herzegovina. It is the smallest of the three with just 5 stores and 1 production factory in Nuem on the coast of the Adriatic Sea.

H/CF has a mature Enterprise Architecture team that has been in existence for 4 years and has performed many successful projects using the TOGAF® model. But this will be the first time that they have attempted a merging of a new entity into the enterprise. One of the concerns of the stakeholders is the state of Yakovich's Security Architecture. Since H/CL is uninformed about Bosnian regulations and Yankovich's own security practices, they want to make sure that this is given a high-level of scrutiny by the EA organization.

QUESTION

Refer to the scenario

You are the Lead EA. Based on TOGAF® 9, which of the following is the best answer?

ANSWERS

M. Consolidate the company's information systems into a single domain to reduce the task of security policy development to a manageable size. Information objects should be transferred within the information domain in accordance with established rules, conditions, and procedures expressed in the security policy in the domain. Analyze minimum-security requirements to ensure that absolute protection will be achieved for the information domain across communications. Security-critical functions will be isolated into relatively small modules that are related in well-defined ways. The operating system will isolate multiple security contexts from each other using hardware protection features. Untrusted software will use end-system resources only by invoking security-critical functions through the separation kernel. Create security associations to form an interactive distributed security context. Standardize security management functions, data structures, and protocols.

N. Break down the company's information systems down into domains to reduce the task of security policy development to a manageable size. Information objects should be transferred between two information domains accordance with established rules, conditions, and procedures expressed in the security policy of each information domain. Analyze minimum-security requirements to ensure that absolute protection will be achieved for each information domain across communications. Security-critical functions will be isolated into relatively small modules that are related in well-defined ways. The operating system will isolate multiple security contexts from each other using hardware protection features. Untrusted software will use end-system resources only by invoking security-critical functions through the separation kernel. Create security associations to form an interactive distributed security context. Standardize security management functions, data structures, and protocols.

O. Consolidate the company's information systems into a single technology domain to reduce the task of security policy development to a manageable size. Hardware should be transferred within the technology domain in accordance with established rules, conditions, and procedures expressed in the security and data transfer policies in the domain. Analyze minimum-security requirements to ensure that relative protection will be achieved for the technology domain across communications. Hardware-critical functions will be isolated into relatively small modules that are related in well-defined ways. The operating system will isolate a single security context using hardware protection features. Untrusted personnel will use end-system resources only by invoking security-critical functions through the separation kernel. Create communication associations to form an interactive distributed security context. Standardize security management functions, data structures, and protocols.

P. Conduct a risk assessment to classify and identify potential security risks, and produce a Risk Identification and Mitigation Assessment Worksheet. Initiate an iteration of Requirements Management and, based on the updated security requirements, produce and announce a new official security policy. Create a Codified Data/Information Asset Ownership and Custody Catalog. Conduct an iteration of Phase H to revise change management guidelines using the resulting documentation and a Data Classification Policy Catalog. Gain a complete understanding of the business security requirements; find the pain point of the stakeholders for security constraints; get a clear understanding of what assets need to be protected, from whom they need to be protected, who has authorization to access them and to what level of security they need; document security forensics, perform a threat analysis; and assess the impact of new security measures side effects; determine ''what can go wrong?'

SCENARIO SET #5 ANSWER KEYS

SCENARIO #33 Elegant Solutions 4 U

Topic		Security
Subjects/Rationale		This scenario requires the proper selection of security steps and techniques.
Most Correct	C	This answer follows the guidelines set in Chapter 21 of the TOGAF® book.
Second Best	A	While creating a new security policy would have the same effect, it would be less efficient than a revision.
Third Best	B	The Application/Technology Matrix and Data/Entity Component Catalog are not valid for this scenario; security policies are not developed, written, or published in Phase G.
Distractor	D	Many non-existent artifacts and incorrect selection of Phases.

SCENARIO #34 Basis Computers

Topic		Architecture Maturity Models
Subjects/Rationale		This scenario requires the correct application of ACMM to a business challenge.
Most Correct	A	This answer explains how to apply ACMM to a business challenge.
Second Best	B	Business Scenarios are conducted in Phase A. A Gap analysis must be performed in Phase E before a solution can be created.
Third Best	C	A greenfield solution is not effective in this situation.
Distractor	D	An Implementation Factor Assessment and Deduction Matrix is not a valid tool for this task. This answer does not really approach the concerns.

SCENARIO #35 SASSI

Topic		Security and Risk Management
Subjects/Rationale		Apply Risk and Security Management for addressing cost overruns and IP protection.
Most Correct	B	Follows Part III Sections 21 and 31.
Second Best	A	The answer does not adequately address security concerns.
Third Best	D	The answer does not adequately address risks.
Distractor	C	The answer does not address any of the stakeholder concerns.

SCENARIO #36 Creature Comforts Hospitality

Topic		Stakeholder Management
Subjects/Rationale		Make sure that the proper stakeholders are identified and will buy-in to the new architecture.
Most Correct	D	This answer follows the guidelines and techniques for stakeholder management in the ADM Guidelines and Techniques.
Second Best	B	Stakeholder Management begins in Phase A. Without a Stakeholder Power Grid, you will not be aware which of the stakeholders are pulling along or pushing against the plan.
Third Best	C	Out of proper phases and use of non-related artifacts
Distractor	A	Many issues with this answer.

SCENARIO #37 Bernadi Auto Veloci #1

Topic		Developing a System Engineering View
Subjects/Rationale		The scenarios requires knowledge of developing system engineering views in accordance with Part IV Section 35.7.4
Most Correct	C	Follows the guidelines set in Part IV Section 35.7.3
Second Best	B	Follows many of the aspects, but has some confused elements; compare to the most correct answer.
Third Best	D	Some correct elements and some artifacts may apply, but not directly hitting the mark.
Distractor	A	The answer is not relevant to this scenario.

SCENARIO #38 Bernadi Auto Veloci #2

Topic		Develop Software Engineering Views
Subjects/Rationale		The scenarios requires knowledge of developing software engineering views in accordance with Part IV Section 35.7.3
Most Correct	A	Follows the guidelines set in Part IV Section 35.7.3
Second Best	B	Follows many of the aspects, but has some confused elements; compare to the most correct answer.
Third Best	C	Some correct elements and some artifacts may apply, but not directly hitting the mark.
Distractor	D	The answer is not relevant to this scenario.

SCENARIO #39 Hannitz/Colmburg Fashions #1

Topic		Developing Business Architecture Views
Subjects/Rationale		The scenario calls for the specification of developing a Business Architecture view. Part IV, Section 35.7.1
Most Correct	B	Clearly follows the specifications
Second Best	D	Many of the tasks are correct, but not all relate specifically to Phase B.
Third Best	C	This answer contains many irrelevant tasks from other Phases.
Distractor	A	This answer has no relation to the question.

SCENARIO #40 Hannitz/Colmburg Fashions #2

Topic		Developing an Enterprise Security View
Subjects/Rationale		This scenario sets up a requirement to create an Enterprise Security view.
Most Correct	B	Follows the guidelines set in Part IV, Section 35.7.2
Second Best	A	Reducing the task of security policy development is provided not by consolidating domains, but by breaking them down into many smaller domains. See the Most Correct answer for other details
Third Best	C	Besides the problems above, there are references to elements not related to security as specified in Part IV, Section 35.7.2.
Distractor	D	This answer completely misses the mark.

About the Author

Steve Else, Ph.D., CEO, EA Principals, Inc.

A leading innovator, practitioner/consultant, lecturer, educator, and trainer in Enterprise Architecture (EA) and related topics for nearly two decades, Dr. Steve Else has many roles in the global strategic transformation community. The Founder and CEO of EA Principals, Inc. (EAP) (see http://eaprincipals.com), Steve is one of the leading 10 TOGAF® trainers in the world, having trained about 1750 people himself. He is author of the book, *Organization Theory and Transformation of Large, Complex Organizations*.

In addition to running EAP, he has established and leads the Enterprise and Solution Architecture Institute (ESAII) at (see http://esaii.org), under the Center for Public-Private Enterprise (CPPE) (see http://cppe.org), which he founded in 1998). ESAII expands his professional outreach globally and will also allow for bringing together experts to mentor students on complex, innovative enterprise solutions approaches (going beyond just the enterprise architecture part of value delivery.

Bringing a wealth of practical and academic experience to his EA and TOGAF® and ArchiMate® 2 Certification Training, (certified in both and having trained over 1750 professionals), he is also an ISEB Certified Enterprise and Solutions Architect, a Project Management Professional (PMP®), and a FEAC Certified Enterprise Architect (CEA). Clients have included the U.S. government, the Dubai government, the Portuguese Government; U.S. State governments in Pennsylvania, California, Colorado, and Virginia; GE, HP, Oracle, IBM, American Express, Cap Gemini, Cisco, Master Card, Nokia Siemens Networks, Verizon, Boeing; Fannie Mae, the Bill and Melinda Gates Foundation, and the Howard Hughes Medical Institute, among many others. ESAII offers 3 levels of certification in EA and/or Enterprise Solutions Architecture (ESA) through its global offerings that EAP runs: Associate Certified Enterprise Architect, Certified Enterprise Architect and Master Certified Enterprise Architect or Master Certified Enterprise Solution Architect. In addition, ESAII is the Founder and Executive Editor of the *Enterprise Architecture Professional Journal* (see http://eapj.org).

Steve is committed to helping cross-pollinate best business and technology practices as well as innovation across the government and between the government and the private sector, and other organizations. As part of his work at CPPE, he founded and is executive editor for *The Government Transformation Journal* (see http://cppe.org) and was the Founder and the first Executive Editor (for about 3 years) of *The EA Zone Journal*.

Steve has served in key EA consulting/practitioner roles in both the private and public sectors, including BAE Systems, CSC, Dynamics Research Corporation, and Synectics for Management Decisions in the private sector; and the Departments of Defense, Homeland Security, Transportation, and Health and Human Services in the public sector.

Teaching Enterprise Architecture, Business Intelligence/Analytics, Information Systems Engineering Management, and Systems Engineering at the graduate level is a way Steve also contributes his knowledge and insights. He has also taught Systems Analysis and Design, Technology Forecasting and Assessments, Knowledge Management, International Trade, and IT Project and Change Management over the span of several years.

A passionate participant in EA, IT, and systems engineering professional communities, Steve is the Founder and Chair of the Washington DC Chapter of the Association of Enterprise Architects, and Assistant Director of Knowledge on the Technical Operations Board of the International Council on Systems Engineering (see http://INCOSE.org).

At the time he began Enterprise Architecture about 20 years ago, he was still a career Air Force officer, retiring soon afterwards in Alexandria, VA. In the Air Force, among many exciting missions and tours of duties, he also served as an Assistant Air Attaché in Paris, France, where he won a special medal for his work in the first Iraq War, also receiving a high medal from the French government. In his final assignment at the Pentagon, he was Program Architect for Air Force business transformation, working in the Office of the Chief of Staff. Steve was also an Air Force pilot in numerous aircraft (having started flying when he was 16 and being an instructor pilot at age 19). As an Air Force pilot, he was part of the mission to attempt to free U.S. hostages held in Iran in1979. He also holds an Airline Transport Rating in the Lear Jet and Boeing 717.

4399730R00072

Printed in Great Britain
by Amazon.co.uk, Ltd.,
Marston Gate.